Cooking with
QUINOA

Cooking with
QUINOA
The Supergrain

RENA PATTEN

NEW
HOLLAND

Acknowledgements

To my family Graeme, Christopher, Alex, Lachlan, Kobe, Nikki, Marcus, Madison, and my parents John and Carmelina—thank you for all your love, support, patience and understanding.

To my good friend Romy Hodgson—thank you for your help, constant encouragement, support and loan of your tastebuds.

First published in 2011 by New Holland Publishers (Australia) Pty Ltd
Sydney • Auckland • London • Cape Town

www.newholland.com.au

1/66 Gibbes Street Chatswood NSW 2067 Australia • 218 Lake Road Northcote Auckland New Zealand • 86 Edgware Road London W2 2EA United Kingdom • 80 McKenzie Street Cape Town 8001 South Africa

A record of this book is available at the National Library of Australia

ISBN 9781742570556

Publisher: Linda Williams • Publishing manager: Lliane Clarke • Senior editor: Mary Trewby • Designer: Celeste Vlok • Photographer: Graeme Gillies • Stylist: Kathy McKinnon • Production manager: Olga Dementiev • Printer: Toppan Leefung Printing Limited

10 9 8 7

Contents

What is quinoa?

Quinoa—pronounced keen-wah—is a grain, but not just any grain. It is considered to be almost a complete food, being very high in protein, full of vitamins, gluten- and wheat-free, cholesterol-free, usually organic, of great benefit to everyone—and simply delicious.

An ancient plant native to the Andes mountains in South America, quinoa has been around for over five thousand years and is known to have been a staple food of the Incas. They used it to supplement their diet of potatoes and corn. It was commonly referred to as the 'mother grain' or 'gold of the Incas' and was considered sacred. It is still considered a very important food in the South American kitchen. I refer to quinoa as the 'supergrain of the century'.

Although commonly referred to as a grain (and I do here), in fact quinoa is the seed of a leafy plant called *Chenopodium quinoa* of the Chenopodium (goosefoot) plant family and is distantly related to the spinach plant. Quinoa contains more protein than any grain and this is a complete protein containing all nine amino acids. The quality of this protein has been likened by the World Health Organization as being closest to milk. The amino acid composition is so well balanced and has a particularly high content of the amino acid lysine (which is essential in our diet for tissue repair and growth), making it a must for vegans who may be concerned about the level of protein in their daily diet.

Quinoa is also a very good source of manganese, magnesium, potassium, phosphorous, copper, zinc, vitamins E and B6, riboflavin, niacin and thiamine. It has more calcium than cow's milk, is an excellent antioxidant, is rich in dietary fibre and has more iron than any grain. It also has the highest content of unsaturated fats and a lower ratio of carbohydrates than any other grain, plus a low Glycemic Index level. The health benefits are truly enormous.

In the kitchen, quinoa has a huge range of uses and lends itself beautifully to so many dishes. When cooked, it has a very delicate texture and is excellent in soups and sweets, and makes wonderful salads, pasta, breads and delicious vegetarian and non-vegetarian meals.

It is simple to prepare, easy to digest and most enjoyable to eat. It is very light on the stomach and you don't tend to feel at all heavy after eating a meal made with quinoa. To those who are gluten- and wheat-intolerant, quinoa is a food that can offer you a greater variety and selection of food for your table.

What does it look like?

The grain itself is tiny and round with a fine band around it, ending in what looks like a minute 'tail'. As it cooks, this 'tail' spirals out and almost detaches itself, making an outer white ring that is clearly visible and quite distinct from the rest of the grain. The cooked quinoa is very soft in the centre—although the tail retains a bit of crunch—and has a very delicate texture. It expands to almost four times its original volume.

There are many different varieties of quinoa and it is available in grain form, flakes and flour. The colour of the grain can vary from white (opaque), pale yellow to red, purple, brown and black. It is available at most health food stores or in the health food section of the larger supermarkets.

Cooked quinoa is very distinctive in both taste and appearance with a lovely, slightly nutty taste.

It can be substituted for just about any other grain. You can use it as an accompaniment, as you would use rice for example, or with other ingredients to make up a complete meal. The distinct nutty taste is more pronounced in the flour, giving it quite an earthy aroma. The flour can also be slightly bitter, but I find that can be counterbalanced by other, sweeter ingredients in a recipe. The flakes are great as a substitute for normal breadcrumbs, especially for stuffings and coatings.

Preparing quinoa

Quinoa grows in arid climates, at high altitudes and in very poor soil. It has been suggested that the plant's survival over the centuries could be attributed to a soapy-like substance called 'saponin', which creates a bitter coating on the grain and protects it from harsh high-altitude weather as well as birds and insects.

This bitter soapy coating must be removed before cooking. Although most quinoa comes pre-washed and ready to cook, it is still a good idea to rinse it thoroughly before use to remove any residue of saponin.

Simply place the quinoa in a fine sieve and rinse under cold running water while rubbing it lightly between your finger tips. Drain well and it is ready to cook. Make sure the sieve is very fine because the grains are tiny and will otherwise go straight through. Quinoa cooks very quickly simmered in water, stock, juice or milk. One part quinoa, two parts liquid and ten minutes in the saucepan are usually all the time needed to prepare quinoa as a basic cooked grain. However, you may need to cook the quinoa a little longer if the liquid is denser than water, such as a sauce or milk. And sometimes the darker grains—the red and black varieties—can take a little longer to cook.

It can be cooked in the microwave, although that is not my preferred method—it is a bit fiddly and for me seems to take longer. To cook quinoa in the microwave, place one part quinoa to two parts liquid in a microwave-proof dish and cook on high for seven minutes; stir, then cover with plastic wrap and stand for seven to eight minutes. Depending on your microwave, you may need to vary the cooking time.

For an added nutty taste, you can toast the quinoa before cooking. Rinse and drain the quinoa well, then dry-roast in a small non-stick frying pan. When the grains start to pop, remove the pan from the heat and transfer the quinoa to a saucepan with two parts liquid, bring to the boil, then reduce the heat and simmer, covered, for ten minutes. You may be able to find ready-toasted quinoa in some shops.

You can also sprout quinoa by placing one part of rinsed quinoa with three parts water in a jar with a lid and soak for about two hours; drain and rinse, then return to the jar with the lid on and leave to sprout. You must rinse them at least twice a day. They are very tiny sprouts and should be ready in about three days but must be eaten immediately as they do not last. Use the sprouts in salads.

For salads, you will need to cook the quinoa first and then combine with the other ingredients. My family loves salads made with quinoa and so I tend to cook a large batch of the grain and leave it in the refrigerator to use as I need it. Quinoa cooked in water will keep in the refrigerator for up to a week. For most of the other recipes, the grain is cooked with other ingredients, making them easy, one-pot meals.

SOUPS

Carrot, Ginger, Garlic and Coriander Soup

Serves 4–6

This is a fairly thick soup and a meal on its own—if you prefer a thinner consistency, add extra hot water once cooking is finished.

1 tbsp coriander seeds

2 tbsp olive oil

1 large onion, chopped

4 cloves garlic, chopped

2 tbsp chopped fresh ginger

1kg (2lb 3oz) carrots, peeled and
    thickly sliced

6 cups hot vegetable stock

salt and pepper to taste

80g (3oz) uncooked quinoa grain

1 cup hot water

½ cup chopped fresh coriander
    (cilantro)

fresh lime juice

Dry-roast the coriander seeds in a small non-stick frying pan for about a minute until fragrant. Remove from heat and pound into a powder in a mortar and pestle; set aside.

Heat the oil in a large saucepan and cook the onion until soft. Add the garlic, ginger and ground coriander seeds, and cook 1 minute. Add the carrots, stock, salt and pepper, bring back to the boil and simmer covered for 40–50 minutes, until the carrots are tender.

Place the quinoa in a fine sieve, rinse under cold running water and drain.

Puree the soup, return to the saucepan and add the quinoa and hot water. Bring back to the boil, reduce heat, cover and simmer for 10 minutes

Stir in the fresh coriander and simmer for 5–7 minutes more. Serve with a squeeze of lime juice.

Cream of Lettuce Soup

Serves 6

The cream adds extra richness, but you don't have to include it—instead, add a little lemon juice. The soup freezes very well, but freeze without the cream and stir it in just before serving.

1 large leek, roughly chopped
2 tbsp extra virgin olive oil
1 onion, roughly chopped
1 large cos/romain lettuce
5 cups hot chicken or vegetable
   stock
salt and pepper to taste
½ cup red quinoa grain, rinsed and
   drained
½ cup cream

Wash the leek thoroughly to remove all soil and grit.

Heat the oil in a large saucepan, add the onion and leek and cook until soft.

Remove any rough outer leaves from the lettuce, wash really well, roughly chop and add to pan. Pour in the hot stock, season with salt and pepper and bring to the boil. Reduce the heat, cover, and simmer for 20 minutes. Puree until smooth.

Add the quinoa to the soup. Cover and simmer for another 15–20 minutes. Stir in the cream and serve.

Creamy Coconut Seafood Soup

Serves 6

For convenience, I usually use a bought fresh marinara mix, which includes shelled prawns, calamari, mussels and fish. You may want to remove the curry leaves before serving the soup.

4 cloves garlic

1–2 long red chillies

2 tbsp chopped fresh ginger

1 tbsp ground turmeric

1 tsp garam masala

3 tbsp vegetable oil

2 tsp mustard seeds

1 tsp cumin seeds

2 medium red onions, chopped

good handful of fresh curry leaves

2 x 400g (14oz) cans of coconut
    cream

4 cups hot water

pinch of saffron

¾ cup quinoa grain, rinsed and
    drained

1kg (2lb 3oz) seafood marinara mix

zest of 1 lime

¼ cup coriander (cilantro) leaves

sliced red chillies for serving

fresh lime juice for serving

In a mortar and pestle, pound the garlic, chillies and ginger until a fine paste is formed. Stir in the turmeric and garam masala. Set aside.

Heat the oil in a large saucepan, add the mustard and cumin seeds and cook until they start to pop. Add the onion and cook on low to medium heat for about 5 minutes until soft. Stir in the curry leaves and the garlic and ginger paste and cook for a few seconds. Pour in the coconut cream, water and saffron, bring to the boil, reduce the heat and simmer, covered, for 20 minutes.

Add the quinoa to the soup. Simmer for 5 minutes. Add the seafood and lime zest, bring back to the boil and simmer, covered, on low heat for a further 10–15 minutes.

Stir in the fresh coriander and serve with slices of chillies and a squeeze of lime juice.

Greek Egg and Lemon Meatball Soup

Serves 4–6

MEATBALLS

½ cup quinoa grain, rinsed and
   drained
500g (1lb 2oz) minced beef
1 medium onion, grated
2 cloves garlic, finely grated
1 tbsp chopped flatleaf parsley
1 egg
salt and freshly ground black pepper

SOUP

5 cups water
1 medium onion, finely chopped
1 tomato, finely chopped
1 tbsp butter
2 egg yolks
juice of 1 lemon
salt and freshly ground black pepper

For the meatballs, place the quinoa in a bowl with all the other meatball ingredients and mix until thoroughly combined. Roll and shape into small balls. Set aside.

To make the soup, pour water into a large saucepan, add the onion, tomato and butter, and bring to the boil. Reduce the heat and simmer, covered, for 15 minutes.

Add the meatballs to the soup and simmer for about 20–30 minutes, until the meatballs are cooked. Remove the pan from the heat and cool slightly.

In a small bowl, beat the egg yolks with lemon juice, salt and pepper and slowly mix in about 1 cup of the slightly cooled soup stock.

Gently stir the egg mixture into the soup and keep stirring for 1–2 minutes on low heat until the soup is heated through—if the heat is too high, it will curdle.

Zucchini, Garlic and Parmesan Cheese Soup

Serves 4–6

This is a lovely light soup and ideal as an entrée.

1kg (2lb 3oz) zucchini (courgettes)
2 tbsp extra virgin olive oil
1 large onion, finely chopped
4–5 cloves garlic, finely chopped
6 cups chicken or vegetable stock
salt and freshly ground black pepper
80g (3oz) red quinoa grain, rinsed
  and drained
½ cup chopped flatleaf parsley
4 heaped tbsp grated parmesan
  cheese
2 tbsp chopped chives

Top and tail zucchini, rinse and pat dry. Coarsely grate and set aside.

Heat the olive oil in a large saucepan, add the onion and garlic and cook until soft and transparent. Add the zucchini to the pan with the stock, salt and pepper (taste the saltiness of the stock before adding extra salt). Bring to the boil, reduce the heat, cover and simmer for 30 minutes.

Add the quinoa and parsley and simmer for another 15–20 minutes.

Stir in the parmesan cheese and chives just before serving.

Roasted Tomato and Fennel Soup with Basil and Garlic Pesto

Serves 6–8

This is one of my favourite soups and is absolutely delicious.

1.5kg (3lb 4oz) firm, ripe tomatoes

1 tsp sugar

1 large fennel bulb

2 onions, peeled

1 head garlic, sliced in half

extra virgin olive oil

salt and freshly ground black pepper

4 cups hot chicken or vegetable
    stock

80g (3oz) red quinoa grain, rinsed
    and drained

PESTO

2 cloves garlic

4 tbsp extra virgin olive oil

1 large handful fresh basil leaves

Preheat the oven to 190ºC (375ºF).

Cut the tomatoes into quarters, place in a deep baking dish and sprinkle with the sugar. Cut the fennel and onions in half, then slice and place together on a baking tray with the unpeeled garlic. Drizzle the vegetables with extra virgin olive oil, season with salt and pepper and place in the oven to roast. The fennel and onions will take about 30–40 minutes and the tomatoes 45–55 minutes.

Once cooked, remove the skins from the tomatoes and squeeze the garlic out of its skin; discard the skins. Puree all the vegetables, then place in a saucepan with the stock and bring to the boil.

When the soup begins to boil add the quinoa grain, reduce the heat, cover, and cook on low heat for 15–20 minutes. Meanwhile, make the pesto by blending all the ingredients together.

Remove the soup from the heat and stir in the pesto. Adjust the seasoning and serve with a drizzle of extra virgin olive oil. Alternatively, you can serve the soup as is with a dollop of pesto.

Sweet Potato, Chilli, Basil and Balsamic Vinegar Bean Soup

Serves 4–6

This is a thick and hearty soup. If you find it too thick, just add boiling water until you get the consistency you prefer.

2 tbsp olive oil

1 large onion, chopped

750g (1lb 8oz) kumara (sweet potato), peeled and roughly cubed

2–3 long red or green chillies, seeded and chopped

5 cups vegetable or chicken stock

salt and freshly ground black pepper to taste

80g (3oz) quinoa grain, rinsed and drained

1 x 400g (14oz) can borlotti beans, drained and rinsed

1 handful basil leaves, finely shredded

2–3 tbsp balsamic vinegar

extra chillies for garnish

Heat the oil in a large saucepan and sauté the onion until golden. Add the sweet potato, chillies, stock, salt and pepper (check saltiness of stock before adding any salt). Bring to the boil, reduce the heat, cover, and simmer for about 20 minutes, until the sweet potato is tender.

Puree the soup in a blender and return to the saucepan. Add the quinoa and beans, bring back to the boil, reduce the heat and simmer, covered, for another 10–15 minutes.

Stir in the basil and balsamic vinegar and serve with a dish of finely sliced chillies.

Lentil Soup

Serves 6–8

2 cups red lentils
2 tomatoes, quartered
1 large onion, chopped
2 cloves garlic, chopped
1 bay leaf
1 tbsp olive oil
salt and pepper to taste
9 cups water
½ cup quinoa grain, rinsed and
    drained

GARNISH
¼ cup olive oil
1 medium onion, finely grated
4 cloves garlic, finely grated
3 tsp ground cumin
extra virgin olive oil for serving
lemon juice for serving
red chilli for serving

Pick over lentils and remove any small stones and grit. Rinse under cold running water in a fine sieve until the water runs clear and drain.

Place the lentils in a large saucepan with the tomatoes, onion, garlic, bay leaf, olive oil, salt and pepper and 8 cups of water. Bring to the boil, reduce the heat, cover, and simmer on low for 30–40 minutes, until the lentils are tender and the soup has thickened. Skim off any foam that appears on the surface during the cooking.

Meanwhile cook the quinoa. Place it in a small saucepan with the remaining cup of water. Bring to the boil, reduce the heat and simmer, covered, for 10 minutes. Remove from the heat and set aside.

When the lentils are cooked, take the pan from heat and remove the tomato skins and bay leaf. Puree until smooth.

To prepare the garnish, heat the oil in a frying pan and sauté the onion and garlic until a deep golden colour. Stir in the cumin, cook for 30 seconds, then stir in the cooked quinoa, mix well and check seasoning.

Place soup back on the heat, stir in quinoa mixture, mix well and heat through before serving with a drizzle of extra virgin olive oil, a squeeze of lemon juice and sliced fresh chillies.

Pumpkin, Tomato and Pea Soup

Serves 4–6

This is a thick soup and a meal on its own. I use beef stock because of the richness it adds but you could use vegetable or chicken stock. If the soup is too thick just add some boiling water to thin if necessary.

2 tbsp olive oil

1 tbsp butter

2 medium onions, roughly chopped

1kg (2lb 3oz) butternut pumpkin, peeled and cubed

1 tbsp curry powder

1 x 400g (14oz) can diced tomatoes with juice

1 litre (35fl oz) beef stock

salt and pepper

80g (3oz) quinoa grain, rinsed and drained

1 cup boiling water

1½ cups frozen peas

lemon juice for serving

Heat the oil and butter in a large saucepan. Once the butter has melted, add the onions and sauté until golden. Add the pumpkin and curry powder and cook for 2–3 minutes. Stir in the tomatoes and stock, season with salt and pepper and simmer, covered, for 20–30 minutes, until the pumpkin is cooked. Puree the soup.

Add the quinoa and boiling water to the soup. Bring the soup back to the boil, reduce the heat and simmer, covered, for 10 minutes. Stir in the peas and cook for a further 5 minutes.

Serve with a squeeze of lemon juice.

BREADS
and PASTA

Buttermilk Bread Loaf

Makes 1 loaf

This is quite a dense bread and quick to make. It's not a conventional bread dough, but is more like a cake mixture. Everything is mixed together, poured into the tin and baked without having to wait for the dough to rise.

vegetable oil

1½ cups quinoa flakes, plus extra for loaf tin

2 cups quinoa flour

1½ tsp bicarbonate of soda

4 tsp brown sugar

1½ tsp salt

1½ cups buttermilk

2 eggs

¼ cup water

½–1 tsp red or black quinoa grain

Preheat the oven to 190°C (375°F). Brush a 22 x 15 x 8cm (8½ x 6 x 3in) loaf tin with vegetable oil.

Combine the flour, bicarbonate of soda, sugar and salt in a bowl, then mix in the 1½ cups quinoa flakes. Whisk together the buttermilk, egg and water and slowly incorporate into the dry ingredients, mixing well. This will be a fairly wet mixture.

Pour the bread mixture into the prepared tin, sprinkle the top with quinoa grain and bake for about 60–70 minutes, until the bread is cooked, is deep golden and sounds hollow when tapped.

Herb Bread

Makes 1 round loaf

You can add 1 very finely grated clove of garlic to the bread mixture.

1 cup quinoa flour

1 tsp bicarbonate of soda

1 cup quinoa flakes

½ tsp salt

½ tsp ground paprika

2 tbsp finely chopped fresh chives

1 tbsp finely chopped fresh parsley

1 tsp finely chopped fresh rosemary

1 tsp fresh thyme leaves

2 tbsp extra virgin olive oil

1 cup full-cream milk

Preheat the oven to 180°C (350°F). Grease a 20cm (8in) round cake tin with oil.

Sift the quinoa flour and bicarbonate of soda into a large bowl, add the quinoa flakes, salt, paprika and the herbs. Mix well.

Whisk together the oil and milk and combine with the dry ingredients. This is a fairly wet bread mixture.

Pour the bread mixture into the prepared tin, flatten with the back of a spoon and brush top with a little extra virgin olive oil. Place the bread in the oven and bake for 20–25 minutes until golden. Leave to cool in the tin.

Olive Flat Bread

Makes 1 x 20cm (8in) round loaf

This is a lovely bread to have with soups. You can leave out the olives and oregano and make a plain flat bread.

2 cups quinoa flour
1 tsp bicarbonate of soda
2 tsp sugar
2 tsp sea salt
1 tsp dried oregano
2 tbsp extra virgin olive oil
12–14 black olives, pitted and sliced
1 cup warm water

Preheat the oven to 180°C (350°F). Line a baking tray with baking paper.

Sift the quinoa flour, bicarbonate of soda, sugar and salt into a bowl. Stir in the oregano. Add the olive oil and olives and, with your hands, mix in as much of the water as it takes to make a soft, pliable but not sticky dough. Sprinkle with extra flour if necessary.

Place the dough onto a floured board and lightly knead it to ensure all the olives are evenly distributed. Shape into a disc, approximately 20cm (8in) in diameter, and place on the prepared baking tray. Using a knife, make 3–4 light slashes across the bread. Brush with extra virgin olive oil and sprinkle with extra sea salt.

Place in the oven and bake for about 25–30 minutes, until the bread sounds hollow when tapped.

Cornbread

Serves 6–8

This is excellent with soups or salads.

¾ cup quinoa flour
½ cup quinoa flakes
1 cup polenta
1 tbsp brown sugar
1 tsp bicarbonate of soda
½–1 tsp chilli flakes
4 shallots or spring onions
    (scallions), finely sliced
1 cup frozen corn
salt and freshly ground pepper to
    taste
1¼ cups buttermilk
3 large eggs
80ml (3fl oz) extra light olive oil

Preheat the oven to 180°C (350°F). Brush a 24cm (9½in) square cake tin, preferably non-stick, with oil.

Place the quinoa flour, quinoa flakes, polenta, sugar, bicarbonate of soda and chilli flakes in a large bowl and mix well. Stir in the shallots and corn, and season with salt and pepper.

Whisk together the buttermilk, eggs and olive oil and pour them into the dry ingredients. Mix well.

Pour the batter into the prepared tin and bake for 20–25 minutes, until golden and a skewer comes out clean when tested.

Fresh Pasta Dough

Serves 4

You can use this basic pasta recipe to make sheets for the lasagne recipe (on page 115) or any other pasta shape. Pasta dough can be prepared the day before use and refrigerated. Bring dough back to room temperature for half an hour before rolling and shaping.

500g (16oz) quinoa flour
¼ tsp salt
5 extra large eggs
1 tbsp olive oil

Sift the flour with the salt and place in a mound on a flat surface, such as a kitchen bench, and make a well in the centre. Break the eggs into the well, add the oil and lightly beat together with a fork. Using the fork, slowly start collecting and mixing the flour with the egg. Continue doing this until they are completely blended. At this stage, the dough may look as if it will never come together, but it will. If the dough is too hard and unworkable, add a very little water.

When you can no longer use the fork because the mixture is too stiff, start working and kneading the dough with your hands until it all binds together and you have a smooth and pliable dough. You will need to knead for 10 minutes. The dough may be a little on the stiff side but will soften after resting.

Wrap the dough in plastic and let it rest for about 30 minutes before you start rolling and cutting as per your pasta machine instructions, or by hand. The pasta dough will be dark in colour but lightens as it cooks.

Cook in lots of boiling salted water but watch as this pasta cooks fairly quickly.

Gnocchi

Serves 4–6

1kg (2lb 3oz) brushed potatoes
1 large egg
salt and freshly ground black pepper
1½-2 cups quinoa flour

Line a baking tray with baking paper and lightly dust with quinoa flour.

Boil the potatoes in their skins until tender. Drain and peel. Puree the potatoes while still warm with a ricer, food mill or sieve (you can use a potato masher, but it must be a very fine mash).

Place the potato in a large bowl, mix in the egg, season with salt and pepper and slowly add as much flour as it takes to form a smooth and firm dough. The amount of flour you use will depend on the potatoes used.

Cut the dough into three pieces and, with the palm of your hands, roll each into a long sausage shape. Cut into 2.5cm (1in) pieces and gently run each one down a grater, pressing down with your index finger to roughen the surface—this will help the sauce stick to the gnocchi better. Place the gnocchi on the prepared tray.

Cook the gnocchi in small batches in boiling salted water, lifting them out with a slotted spoon as soon as they rise to the surface.

Serve immediately with your favourite sauce.

SALADS

Mexican Corn and Red Kidney Bean Salad

Serves 4–6

You can use fresh or frozen corn kernels. If using frozen, make sure they are fully thawed and dry before placing in the frying pan to toast.

½ cup quinoa grain, rinsed and
    drained
1 cup water
2 cups fresh corn kernels
½ large red capsicum (pepper), diced
½ large green capsicum (pepper),
    diced
1 small red onion, halved and thinly
    sliced
1 x 400g (14oz) can red kidney
    beans, rinsed and drained
80g (3oz) chopped coriander
    (cilantro)

MEXICAN DRESSING
¼ tsp dried ground oregano
¼ tsp ground cumin
¼ tsp paprika
finely chopped fresh chilli to taste
juice of 1 lime
4 tbsp extra virgin olive oil
salt and freshly ground black pepper
    to taste

Place the quinoa in a small saucepan with the water, bring to the boil, then reduce the heat, cover and simmer for 10 minutes until all the water is absorbed. Remove from the heat and cool completely.

Dry-toast the corn in a non-stick frying pan until it turns golden, then remove from the heat and cool.

Place the quinoa, corn, red and green capsicums, onion, red kidney beans and coriander in a bowl and mix well.

Whisk all the dressing ingredients together and pour over salad. Toss well and serve.

Lentil and Chilli Salad with Lime and Fresh Coriander

Serves 6–8

1 cup quinoa grain, rinsed and
  drained
2 cups water
2 x 400g (14oz) cans brown lentils
1 small red onion, finely chopped
3 shallots or spring onions
  (scallions)
3 long red chillies
½ bunch coriander (cilantro)
salt
juice of 1–1½ limes
4 tbsp extra virgin olive oil

Place the quinoa in a small saucepan with the water, bring to the boil, then reduce the heat, cover and simmer for 10 minutes until all the water is absorbed. Remove from the heat and cool completely.

Rinse and drain the lentils and place in a bowl with the red onion. Top and tail the shallots, leaving quite a bit of the green part, and finely slice diagonally. Add to the bowl with the quinoa and finely sliced chillies (remove seeds if you wish).

Finely chop the stalks of the coriander and roughly chop the leaves; add to the salad. Season with salt to taste. Add the lime juice and olive oil and toss well. Adjust the dressing if necessary.

Place the salad in a serving dish and decorate with extra slices of chilli and coriander leaves.

Roasted Capsicum and Cannellini Bean Salad

Serves 4

This salad can be prepared a few hours in advance to allow all the flavours to combine. I like to drizzle it with a little extra olive oil just before serving.

¾ cup quinoa grain, rinsed and
   drained
1½ cups water
2 x 400g (14oz) cans cannellini
   beans
350g (12½oz) roasted red capsicum
   (pepper), cut into pieces
½ cup chopped flatleaf parsley
3 tbsp chopped chives
½ cup black olives, pitted and halved
3 tbsp extra virgin olive oil
2 tbsp lemon juice
1 tbsp Dijon mustard
salt and freshly ground black pepper

Place the quinoa in a small saucepan with the water. Bring to the boil, then reduce the heat, cover and simmer for 10 minutes until all the water is absorbed. Remove from the heat and cool completely.

Lightly rinse and drain the beans, then place in a bowl with the capsicums, parsley, chives and olives. Add the cooled quinoa and season with salt and pepper to taste.

Whisk together the olive oil, lemon juice, mustard, salt and pepper, pour over the salad, toss well and serve.

Beetroot Garden Salad

Serves 6–10

This salad is an all-time favourite and looks stunning on a white platter. It's great for barbeques. Home-cooked beetroot is best to use and well worth the effort. If you must use the tinned variety, whole beetroot is better than the slices.

¾ cup quinoa grain, rinsed and
    drained

1½ cups water

500g (1lb 2oz) cooked beetroot, diced

2 celery stalks, finely sliced

½ capsicum (pepper), diced

1 medium carrot, finely diced

1 large red onion, finely chopped

4 shallots or spring onions
    (scallions), finely sliced

2–3 radishes, finely sliced

1 x 400g (14oz) can cannellini beans,
    rinsed and drained

1 generous cup roughly chopped
    flatleaf parsley

DRESSING

1 clove garlic

salt and freshly ground black pepper
    to taste

2 tbsp red wine vinegar

5 tbsp extra virgin olive oil

Place the quinoa in a small saucepan with the water, bring to the boil, then reduce the heat, cover and simmer for 10 minutes until all the water is absorbed. Remove from the heat and cool completely. Place the cooled quinoa in a large bowl with all other salad ingredients.

To make dressing, place the garlic, seasoning, vinegar and olive oil in a mortar and pestle and pound until blended or very finely grate the garlic and mix with the other ingredients. Adjust quantities to taste. Pour over the salad and toss gently to combine.

Pancetta, Mushroom and Zucchini Salad

Serves 6–10

You can substitute bacon for the pancetta. I prefer to use pancetta as it has all those wonderful spices through it.

¾ cup quinoa grain, rinsed and drained

1½ cups water

500g (1lb 2oz) mushrooms

500g (1lb 2oz) zucchini (courgettes)

extra virgin olive oil

125g (4oz) pancetta, sliced

3 large cloves garlic, peeled and sliced

½ cup basil leaves, torn into small pieces

½–1 red chilli, seeded and finely chopped

2 tbsp extra virgin olive oil

2 tbsp red wine vinegar

sea salt and freshly ground black pepper

shaved parmesan cheese

Place the quinoa in a small saucepan with the water, bring to the boil, then reduce heat, cover and simmer for 10 minutes until all the water is absorbed. Remove from heat and cool.

Trim a little of the stalk from the mushrooms and cut vertically into thickish slices. Thickly slice the zucchini diagonally.

Heat a griddle pan to hot, brush with a little extra virgin olive oil and grill the mushrooms and zucchini until golden but still a little firm. Remove from the pan, cool completely and place in a bowl.

Cut each pancetta slice into 4 pieces; add to griddle pan with the garlic, cook 1–2 minutes until the pancetta is lightly crisp and the garlic fragrant. Take care the garlic doesn't burn.

Add the pancetta and garlic to the mushrooms and zucchini with the quinoa, basil and chilli.

Whisk the olive oil with the red wine vinegar, add salt and pepper to taste. Pour the dressing over salad and toss well. Scatter through the shaved parmesan and serve.

Tabouleh

Serves 6–8

Traditionally tabouleh is made out of cracked wheat (burghul) which means if you have a gluten/wheat intolerance you would not be able to eat it. By using quinoa, it can be enjoyed by everyone, plus I think it has more eye appeal.

1 cup quinoa grain, rinsed and
    drained
2 cups water
2 firm ripe tomatoes
2–3 cups chopped flatleaf parsley
1 red onion, finely chopped
4 shallots or spring onions
    (scallions), sliced
2 Lebanese cucumbers, diced
juice of ½–1 lemon
80g (3oz) extra virgin olive oil
salt and freshly ground black pepper
    to taste

Place the quinoa in a small saucepan with the water, bring to the boil, then reduce the heat, cover and simmer for 10 minutes until all the water is absorbed. Remove from heat and cool completely.

Slice, deseed and dice the tomatoes, place into a large bowl with the cooled quinoa, parsley, onion, shallots and cucumber. Toss well. Add the lemon juice and olive oil, season with salt and pepper and toss to thoroughly combine. If possible, allow to stand for 30 minutes before serving.

Salami, Roasted Peppers, Sundried Tomato and Olive Salad

Serves 4–6

For a vegetarian option, leave out the salami. I tend to add anchovies as I absolutely love them and they go so well in this salad.

¾ cup quinoa grain, rinsed and
    drained
1½ cups water
250g (8oz) mushrooms, sliced
3 shallots or spring onions
    (scallions), sliced
125g (4oz) sundried tomatoes, sliced
125g (4oz) roasted capsicum
    (peppers), sliced
2 tbsp capers, drained
24 kalamata olives, pitted
125g (4oz) salami, cut into pieces
1 clove garlic, very finely grated
½ cup chopped basil
½ cup chopped flatleaf parsley
2 tbsp balsamic vinegar
4–5 tbsp extra virgin olive oil
salt and freshly ground black pepper

Place the quinoa in a small saucepan with the water, bring to the boil, then reduce the heat, cover and simmer for 10 minutes until all the water is absorbed. Remove from heat and cool completely.

Place the cooled quinoa in a large bowl with all other ingredients. Toss well and let all the flavours combine for about 30 minutes before serving.

Tomato, Basil and Garlic Salad

Serves 4

This is a very simple and quick salad to prepare. For an even brighter salad, you could mix in some orange cherry or grape tomatoes if you can find them.

¾ cup quinoa grain, rinsed and
    drained
1½ cups water
250g (8oz) red cherry or grape
    tomatoes
250g (8oz) yellow cherry or grape
    tomatoes
¾–1 cup torn basil leaves
1–2 cloves garlic, very finely grated
1½ tbsp balsamic vinegar
3 tbsp extra virgin olive oil
sea salt and freshly ground black
    pepper

Place the quinoa in a small saucepan with the water, bring to the boil, then reduce the heat, cover and simmer for 10 minutes until all the water is absorbed. Remove from the heat and cool completely.

Cut the tomatoes in half and place into a large salad bowl with the basil, garlic and cooled quinoa.

Whisk the vinegar with the olive oil and add salt and pepper to taste. Pour over the salad and toss well.

Prawn and Avocado Salad

Serves 4–6

This is a lovely summer salad that can also be served as an entrée.

¾ cup red quinoa grain, rinsed and
    drained
1½ cups water
750g (1lb 10oz) cooked prawns
2 stalks celery, finely sliced
½ cup chopped flatleaf parsley
2 long red chillies, sliced
2 large avocados, peeled and cut into
    chunks
¼ cup extra virgin olive oil
2 tbsp balsamic vinegar
salt to taste

Place the quinoa in a small saucepan with the water, bring to the boil, then reduce the heat, cover and simmer for 10 minutes until all the water is absorbed. Remove from the heat and cool completely.

Peel and devein prawns, leaving the tails intact. Place in a large bowl with the quinoa, celery, parsley, chillies and avocados and gently toss to combine.

Mix the olive oil, vinegar and salt together, pour over the salad and toss well. Allow the flavours to combine for about 30 minutes before serving. Adjust dressing to suit your taste if necessary.

Fattoush Salad

Serves 6–8

Sumac and zatar are seasonings that are widely used in Middle Eastern cooking and can be found at most delicatessens. Fattoush salad is traditionally served with pita bread that is crisped in the oven, broken up and mixed into the salad. Here quinoa is used instead of the bread, making it suitable for people with gluten and wheat intolerances

¾ cup red quinoa grain, rinsed and
   drained
1½ cups water
2 Lebanese cucumbers
250g (8oz) cherry tomatoes, halved
1 red onion, finely chopped
4 shallots or spring onions
   (scallions), sliced
½ large red capsicum (pepper), diced
½ large green capsicum (pepper),
   diced
4 radishes, sliced
½ cup roughly chopped mint
½ cup roughly chopped flatleaf
   parsley
½ cup roughly chopped coriander
   (cilantro)
3 tbsp lemon juice
4 tbsp extra virgin olive oil
3 tsp sumac seasoning
1 tsp zatar seasoning
salt and freshly ground black pepper.

Place the quinoa in a small saucepan with the water, bring to the boil, then reduce the heat, cover and simmer for 10 minutes until all the water is absorbed. Remove from the heat and cool completely.

Cut the cucumbers into four lengthways, then dice. Place in a large salad bowl, add the quinoa and all the remaining ingredients and toss well.

This can be served as a side dish or as a main meal.

Chicken Salad

Serves 4 as a main
meal

2 chicken breast fillets

1 cup quinoa grain, rinsed and
   drained

2 cups chicken stock or water

3 tbsp chopped parsley

2 tbsp chopped chives

1 tsp finely chopped rosemary

20 black kalamata olives, pitted and
   halved

1 punnet cherry tomatoes cut in half

2 tbsp balsamic vinegar

4 tbsp extra virgin olive oil

1 generous tbsp horseradish cream

salt and freshly ground black pepper

Preheat the oven to 170ºC (325ºF).

Rub the chicken breasts with a little olive oil and season with salt and pepper. Place on a baking tray and roast in the oven for about 15 minutes, until cooked. Remove from the oven, cover with foil and allow to rest.

Place the quinoa in a small saucepan with the stock or water, bring to the boil, then reduce the heat, cover and simmer for 10 minutes until all the water is absorbed. Remove from the heat and cool completely.

When the quinoa has cooled, place it in a salad bowl. Using two forks, shred the chicken into bite-sized pieces and add to the bowl with the parsley, chives, rosemary and olives. Gently squeeze out the seeds from the cherry tomatoes and add the tomato flesh to the bowl .

Whisk the vinegar, olive oil, horseradish cream, salt and pepper together, pour over into the salad, toss gently and serve.

Mediterranean Vegetable Salad

Serves 8–10

This is one of those salads that you can eat as a meal on its own or as a side dish. It's great for barbeques or a party as it really feeds a crowd.

½ cup red quinoa grain, rinsed and
  drained
½ cup white quinoa grain, rinsed
  and drained
2 cups water
1 cup cooked peas
1 cup cooked green beans, chopped
  into large pieces
1 cup cooked corn kernels
2 medium carrots, peeled and grated
½ red capsicum (pepper), deseeded
  and diced
½ green capsicum (pepper),
  deseeded and diced
250g (8oz) cherry tomatoes, halved
1 medium red onion, finely chopped
4 shallots or spring onions
  (scallions), finely sliced
DRESSING
80g (3oz) extra virgin olive oil
1 clove garlic, finely grated
1 tsp Dijon mustard
2 tbsp red wine vinegar
salt and freshly ground black pepper

Place the red and white quinoa in a small saucepan with the water, bring to the boil, then reduce the heat, cover and simmer for 10 minutes until all the water is absorbed. Remove from the heat and cool completely.

In a salad bowl, place the peas, beans, corn, carrots, capsicum, tomatoes, onion and shallots. Mix together and add the cooled quinoa.

For the dressing, whisk together the olive oil, garlic, mustard, vinegar and seasoning and pour over the salad. Toss well and leave for at least 30 minutes before serving to allow the flavours to combine.

Mediterranean Summer Salad

Serves 4–6

This is a lovely salad and great as an accompaniment with meat or fish. You can roast your own capsicums or buy them ready roasted or chargrilled. The anchovies add an extra zing to the dressing but you can leave them out. This has all the true flavours of the Mediterranean.

¾ cup quinoa grain, rinsed and
   drained
1½ cups water
½ cup pitted black kalamata olives
2 tbsp capers, drained
125g (4oz) sun-dried tomatoes, sliced
150g (5oz) roasted capsicums
   (peppers), cut into chunks
280g (9oz) artichoke hearts, quartered
1 x 400g (14oz) can borlotti beans,
   rinsed and drained
1 green chilli, seeded and chopped
1 small red onion, finely chopped
2 tbsp chopped chives
½ cup chopped dill

DRESSING
2 anchovy fillets (optional)
4 tbsp extra virgin olive oil
1½–2 tbsp red wine vinegar
2 cloves garlic
salt and freshly ground black
   pepper to taste

Place the quinoa in a small saucepan with the water, bring to the boil, then reduce the heat, cover and simmer for 10 minutes until all the water is absorbed. Remove from the heat and cool completely.

Halve the olives lengthways and place in a large bowl with quinoa, capers, sun-dried tomatoes, capsicums, artichokes, beans, chilli, onion and herbs. Mix thoroughly.

For the dressing, place the anchovies, olive oil, vinegar, garlic and seasoning in a blender or mortar and pestle and whiz or grind together until blended.

Pour the dressing over the salad, check the seasoning (you will need to add salt if not using the anchovies). Chill for about 30 minutes before serving.

Thai Beef Salad

Serves 4

You can use fresh or frozen corn kernels. If using frozen, make sure they are fully thawed and dry before placing in the frying pan to toast.

90g (3oz) dried mushrooms

½ cup quinoa grain, rinsed and
   drained

1 cup water

500g (1lb 2oz) rump steak

olive oil

1 small red onion, finely sliced

2 shallots or spring onions
   (scallions), sliced diagonally

½ red capsicum (pepper), deseeded
   and thinly sliced

1 good handful of bean sprouts

125g (4oz) green beans, cooked and
   chopped into large pieces

1 Lebanese cucumber, quartered
   lengthways and diced

1 green chilli, thinly sliced

1 red chilli, thinly sliced

1 cup coriander (cilantro) leaves,
   tightly packed

DRESSING

¼ cup fish sauce

juice of 1–2 limes

2 cloves garlic, finely grated

Place the mushrooms in a bowl, cover with boiling water and let stand for 15 minutes. Drain and squeeze dry, then slice and set aside.

Meanwhile, place the quinoa in a small saucepan with the water, bring to the boil, then reduce the heat, cover and simmer for 10 minutes until all the water is absorbed. Remove from the heat and cool completely.

Rub the steak on both sides with the oil and season with salt and pepper. Heat a griddle or frying pan until very hot, add the steak and cook on both sides, until medium rare. Remove from pan, cover with foil, allow to rest and then cut into strips.

Place the onion, shallots, capsicum, bean sprouts, beans, cucumber, chillies and coriander in a bowl (remove the seeds from the chillies if you don't want too much heat). Add the mushrooms, quinoa and steak.

To make the dressing, mix together the fish sauce, lime juice and garlic, adjusting the amount of lime juice to taste.

Just before serving, pour the dressing over the salad and toss well.

VEGETARIAN

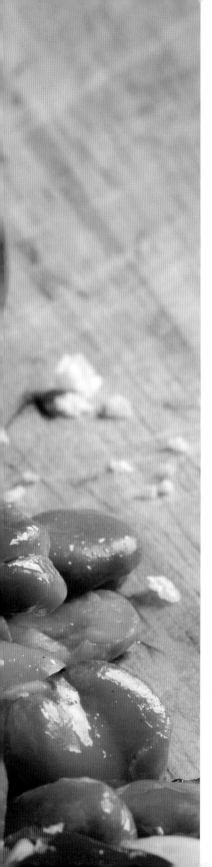

Mushroom and Garlic 'Risotto'

Serves 2–4

This is very quick to prepare. It is like a risotto but you don't have to stand over the stove stirring constantly.

500g (1lb 2oz) mushrooms
3 tbsp olive oil
3–4 cloves garlic, finely chopped
salt and freshly ground black pepper
1 cup quinoa grain, rinsed and
    drained
2 cups hot water
½ cup chopped fresh flatleaf parsley
1 tbsp butter (optional)

Wipe the mushrooms with a damp cloth to remove any dirt then slice thinly. Heat the olive oil in a large frying pan, add the mushrooms and cook until they are tender. Stir in the garlic, salt and pepper.

Add the quinoa to the pan with the water and parsley. Stir well, bring to the boil, then reduce the heat and simmer for 10–15 minutes.

For added richness, stir in the butter before serving.

Eggplant with Chickpeas

Serves 4

4 tbsp olive oil

1 eggplant (aubergine), approx 500g
    (1lb 2oz), cubed

1 large onion, finely chopped

3 cloves garlic, finely chopped

1½ tsp ground cumin

1 tsp ground turmeric

1 tsp chilli flakes

2 ripe tomatoes, skinned and
    chopped

2½ cups hot water

salt

1 cup quinoa grain, rinsed and
    drained

2 x 400g (14oz) cans chickpeas,
    rinsed and drained

zest of 1 lime or lemon

a handful of chopped coriander
    (cilantro), including stalks

Greek yoghurt for serving (optional)

lime or lemon juice for serving

Heat the olive oil in a large frying pan and cook the eggplant until golden. Add the onion and continue cooking until it is soft. You may need to add a little more oil as the eggplant tends to absorb it quickly. Stir in the garlic, cumin, turmeric and chilli and cook for about 30 seconds.

Add the tomatoes and 1 cup of hot water, season with salt, cover and simmer on low heat for 10 minutes. Add the quinoa to the pan with the chickpeas, lime or lemon zest and extra water, bring back to the boil, cover, then reduce the heat and simmer for 10–15 minutes.

Stir in the coriander and cook for another 2–3 minutes. Serve with some Greek yoghurt and/or a squeeze of lime or lemon juice.

Tomato and Basil Baked Capsicums

Serves 2 as a main dish, 4 as entrée

Cut a very fine slice off the bottom of each capsicum if they do not sit straight on the baking dish. Just be careful not to cut right through.

½ cup quinoa grain, rinsed and drained
1 cup water
2 large red capsicums (peppers)
250g (8oz) cherry tomatoes, halved
2 cloves garlic, finely chopped
½ cup chopped basil leaves
2 tbsp capers
2 tbsp balsamic vinegar, plus extra for serving
5 tbsp extra virgin olive oil, plus extra for serving
sea salt and freshly ground black pepper

Preheat the oven to 180°C (350°F).

Place the quinoa in a small saucepan with the water, bring to the boil, then reduce the heat, cover and simmer for 10 minutes until all the water is absorbed. Remove from the heat and cool completely.

Cut the capsicums in half lengthways, leaving the stalks intact, and remove the seeds and excess membrane. Place on a baking tray.

For the filling, place quinoa in a large bowl with the remaining ingredients and mix well. Pile the filling into the capsicums and bake for 20–30 minutes, until the capsicums are soft and tender.

Drizzle with a little balsamic vinegar and extra virgin olive oil before serving. Can be eaten warm or cold.

Moroccan Pumpkin Halves

Serves 4–6

I love the look of these on a platter—they look and taste very special.

1 whole butternut pumpkin, about
   2kg (4.4lb)

3½ tbsp olive oil

salt and pepper

45g (1½oz) pine nuts

2 leeks, cleaned and finely sliced

3 large cloves garlic

1 tsp grated ginger

1½ tsp ground cumin

1tsp ground paprika

1 tsp ground turmeric

1 tsp chilli flakes

1 red capsicum (pepper), deseeded
   and chopped

2 zucchini (courgettes), cubed

salt and freshly ground black pepper

1¾ cups water

1 cup quinoa grain, rinsed and
   drained

2–3 tbsp coriander (cilantro),
   chopped

Preheat the oven to 175°C (340°F).

Cut pumpkin in half lengthways and remove seeds. With a small but sturdy knife carefully remove the pumpkin flesh, creating a bowl with a border about 1.5cm (¾in) thick to hold the filling. Cut a very thin slice off the bottom of each pumpkin half so it sits flat on the tray.

Brush the inside and edges of the pumpkin with a little olive oil and season lightly with salt and pepper. Place on a baking tray and bake for 20–25 minutes until tender.

Dry-roast the pine nuts in a small non-stick frying pan and set aside.

Heat 3 tbsp olive oil in a large frying pan and sauté the leeks until soft, add the garlic and ginger and cook for about 1 minute. Stir in the cumin, paprika, turmeric and chilli, and cook for another 30 seconds. Add the capsicum, zucchini, salt, pepper and 1 cup of water. Stir and simmer, covered, for 10 minutes.

Add the quinoa to the pan with ¾ cup of water. Cover and simmer for another 10-12 minutes. Stir in the coriander and toasted pine nuts. Spoon the mixture into the pumpkin halves. Return to the oven and bake for 10–15 minutes until golden.

Vegetable Bake

Serves 4–6

1 eggplant (aubergine), about 450g
 (1lb)

3 medium zucchini (courgettes)

2 small carrots

2 leeks, washed well

4 cloves garlic, peeled and sliced

extra virgin olive oil

salt and pepper

½ cup quinoa grain, rinsed and
 drained

1 cup water

350g (12½oz) broccoli cut into
 florets

1 tbsp fresh thyme

CHEESE SAUCE

3 tbsp butter

4 tbsp quinoa flour

2¾ cups milk

¾ cup grated tasty cheese

1 tbsp grated parmesan cheese

salt and pepper

ground paprika

extra grated cheese

Preheat the oven to 175ºC (340°F).

Slice the eggplant into three lengthways and then cube. Cut the zucchini, carrots and leek in half then thickly slice. Place the vegetables in a tray with the garlic, drizzle liberally with extra virgin olive oil and season with salt and pepper. Bake for 30–35 minutes, turning the vegetables once or twice during the cooking time.

Meanwhile, place quinoa in a saucepan with the water. Bring to the boil, reduce the heat and simmer, covered, for 10 minutes until all the water is absorbed. Remove from heat and set aside. Boil or steam the broccoli until tender and place in a baking dish with the roasted vegetables, cooked quinoa and thyme.

To make the cheese sauce, melt the butter in a saucepan, stir in the flour to form a roux and cook for a few seconds. Slowly pour in the milk, stirring constantly until the sauce starts to bubble and thicken. Add the tasty and parmesan cheeses and stir until they have melted and the sauce is thick. Season to taste.

Pour two-thirds of the cheese sauce over the vegetables and gently mix to combine all the ingredients together. Adjust the seasoning, then pour remaining sauce on top, sprinkle with extra cheese and paprika. Bake for 20–25 minutes until golden.

Sweet Potato and Zucchini Pie

Serves 4–6

1 cup quinoa grain, rinsed and
    drained
2 cups water
2 tbsp olive oil
1 medium onion, finely chopped
2 cloves garlic, finely chopped
400g (14oz) zucchini (courgette),
    coarsely grated
500g (1lb 2oz) orange sweet potato,
    cooked and mashed
4 eggs
1 cup grated tasty cheese
salt and pepper
1–2 tomatoes, thickly sliced

Preheat the oven to 180°C (350°F).

Place quinoa in a small saucepan with the water. Bring to the boil, reduce the heat and simmer for 10 minutes until all the water is absorbed.

Heat the oil in a small frying pan and sauté the onion until soft and golden, then place in a large bowl. Add the cooked quinoa, garlic, zucchini, sweet potato, lightly beaten eggs, cheese, salt and pepper and mix to thoroughly combine.

Pour the mixture into a greased ovenproof dish and arrange the slices of tomato on top. Bake for 30–40 minutes until the pie is set and browned on the top.

Stuffed Tomatoes with Dill and Pine Nuts

Serves 6

12 medium–large, firm but ripe
    tomatoes
salt
3 tbsp olive oil
1 large onion, finely chopped
45g (1½oz) pine nuts
1½ cups quinoa grain, rinsed and
    drained
1½ cups hot water
3 tbsp chopped dill
2 tbsp chopped parsley
salt and pepper

SAUCE

1 x 400g (14oz) can diced tomatoes
1 tbsp extra virgin olive oil
salt and pepper
1 tbsp chopped parsley
1 tbsp chopped dill
¼ cup water

Preheat the oven to 180°C (350°F).

Cut a slice off the top of each tomato to use as a lid. Using a teaspoon, gently scoop out the pulp and reserve. Sprinkle the inside of each tomato with a little salt and turn upside down onto a wire rack to drain off the excess moisture.

Strain the juices from the pulp and chop the fleshy part; reserve. Discard the seeds.

Heat the olive oil in a large frying pan and sauté the onion 3–4 minutes, until soft. Add the pine nuts and continue sautéing until the onion is golden and the pine nuts have a little colour.

Add the quinoa to the pan, stir well and cook for about 1 minute. Stir in the tomato pulp and juice and cook another minute. Add the water, 3 tbsp of dill, 2 tbsp of parsley, salt and pepper. Stir well, cover and simmer on low heat for 10 minutes. Remove from heat and cool slightly.

To make the sauce, mix all the sauce ingredients together and pour in the bottom of a baking dish.

Fill each tomato with the quinoa mixture and place in the baking dish. Place the tomato lid on top, drizzle with extra virgin olive oil and bake for 20–30 minutes, until cooked.

Stuffed Capsicums with Herbs and Olives

Serves 4

1 cup quinoa grain, rinsed and
   drained
2 cups water
2 red capsicums (peppers)
2 green capsicums (peppers)
1 medium red onion, finely chopped
2 cloves garlic, finely chopped
3 ripe tomatoes, peeled and chopped
2 tbsp chopped parsley
2 tbsp chopped basil
1 tbsp dried oregano leaves
12 black olives, pitted and chopped
freshly ground black pepper
1 cup water
extra virgin olive oil

Place the quinoa in a saucepan with the water. Bring to the boil, then reduce heat, cover and simmer for 10 minutes until all the water is absorbed.

Cut the capsicums in half lengthways, keeping the stalk intact, and remove seeds and membranes.

For the stuffing, mix together the cooked quinoa, onion, garlic, tomatoes, herbs, olives and pepper. Spoon the stuffing mixture into the capsicum halves and place in a baking dish. Pour about 2cm of water into the bottom of the dish and drizzle the capsicums liberally with extra virgin olive oil. Bake for 30–40 minutes until the capsicums are tender and the stuffing is golden.

Middle Eastern Bean Patties with Yoghurt and Mint Sauce

Makes 8–10 patties

½ cup quinoa grain, rinsed and
  drained
1 cup water
2 x 400g (14oz) cans red kidney
  beans
3 cloves garlic, grated
4 shallots or spring onions
  (scallions), finely sliced
1 tsp ground cumin
½–1 tsp chilli powder
3 tbsp chopped coriander
1 egg
salt to taste
2 tbsp olive oil

YOGHURT SALSA
½ cup Greek yoghurt
1 tbsp finely chopped mint
1 tsp extra virgin olive oil
salt and pepper to taste

Place the quinoa in a small saucepan with the water. Bring to the boil, then reduce the heat, cover and simmer for 10 minutes until all the water is absorbed. Remove from the heat and cool.

Rinse and drain the red kidney beans and coarsely mash with fork or potato masher and place in a bowl. Add the cooked quinoa, garlic, shallots, cumin, chilli, coriander and egg, season with salt and mix until all the ingredients are well combined. Divide the mixture into 8 or 10 and shape into round patties.

Heat the olive oil in a non-stick frying pan over medium heat. Add the patties and cook until golden on both sides, about 3–4 minutes each side.

To make the sauce, mix together the yoghurt, mint and extra virgin olive oil, and season with salt and pepper if you wish.

Serve the bean patties with the yoghurt mint sauce and a garden salad.

Mango, Sweet Potato and Tomato Curry

Serves 6

I have used tinned mangoes so that you can prepare this lovely curry all year round. If in season use two fresh mangoes instead.

2 tbsp olive oil
1 tbsp black mustard seeds
1 large onion, halved and thinly sliced
1 tbsp ground turmeric
2 tbsp curry powder
5 cardamom pods, lightly crushed
a small handful fresh curry leaves
4 cloves garlic, chopped
1 tbsp grated fresh ginger
1 long red or green chilli, deseeded
    and sliced
2 x 400g (14oz) cans cherry
    tomatoes, with juice
1 x 400g (14oz) can coconut milk
500g (1lb 2oz) orange sweet potato,
    peeled and cubed
1 cup quinoa grain, rinsed and
    drained
½ cup hot water
1 x 800g (26oz) can mangoes in
    natural juice, drained
½ cup chopped coriander (cilantro)
lime juice for serving

Heat the oil in a large saucepan, add the mustard seeds and cook until they start to pop. Add the onion and cook until it softens. Stir in the turmeric, curry powder, cardamom and curry leaves and cook for a few seconds. Add the garlic, ginger, chilli and salt and cook for a few seconds more, until fragrant.

Stir in the tomatoes, coconut milk and sweet potato, bring to the boil, then reduce heat and simmer, covered, for about 10 minutes, until the potato begins to soften. Stir in the quinoa and water and simmer on low heat for a further 15–20 minutes, until both the potato and quinoa are cooked.

Cut the mangoes into pieces, add to the pan and heat through. Stir in the coriander, squeeze over some lime juice and serve garnished with extra coriander leaves.

Cherry Tomato and Butter Bean Stew

Serves 2–4

This dish can also be eaten cold as a salad.

3 tbsp olive oil
1 large onion, finely chopped
3 cloves garlic, finely chopped
500g (1lb 2oz) cherry tomatoes
½ cup white wine
1–2 tbsp thyme leaves
3 tbsp chopped parsley
salt and pepper
1 cup quinoa grain, rinsed and
   drained
2 x 400g (14oz) cans butter beans,
   rinsed and drained
1½ cups hot water
3 tbsp chopped chives
extra virgin olive oil to serve

Heat the olive oil in a large frying pan and sauté the onion until is soft and starts to change colour. Stir in the garlic and tomatoes and cook for about 5 minutes on medium heat, stirring occasionally, until the tomatoes start to soften. Add the wine and deglaze the pan. Stir in the thyme and parsley and season with salt and pepper.

Add the quinoa to the pan with the beans and water. Bring to the boil, then reduce the heat, cover and simmer for 10–15 minutes, until quinoa is cooked.

Stir in the chives and serve with a good drizzle of extra virgin olive oil.

Zucchini and Olive Bake

Serves 2–4

½ cup quinoa grain, rinsed and
   drained
1 cup water
4 shallots or spring onions
   (scallions), sliced
1 red onion, finely chopped
18 black kalamata olives, pitted and
   chopped
1 red capsicum (peppers), seeded and
   chopped
2 medium zucchini (courgettes),
   coarsely grated
2 large eggs
1 tsp dried oregano
salt and freshly ground black pepper

Preheat the oven to 170ºC (325ºF). Lightly oil a shallow baking dish.

Place the quinoa in a small saucepan with the water. Bring to the boil, then reduce the heat and simmer for 10 minutes until all the water is absorbed. Remove from the heat and cool slightly.

Place quinoa in a large bowl with all other ingredients and mix to combine. Spoon in the mixture into the baking dish and bake for about 20–30 minutes, until set and golden on top.

Allow to stand for 5–10 minutes before serving.

Spinach and Tomato 'Risotto'

Serves 4

My family loves this served with a sprinkling of lemon juice. We don't always have it with parmesan but always with lemon juice.

3 tbsp extra virgin olive oil
1 medium onion, finely chopped
1 tbsp tomato paste
1 x 400g (14oz) can diced tomatoes,
    with juice
1 cup quinoa grain, rinsed and
    drained
2 cups hot water
salt and freshly ground black pepper
350g (12½oz) fresh baby spinach
    leaves, washed
shaved parmesan cheese (optional)

Heat the olive oil in a saucepan and cook the onions until soft and lightly browned. Stir in tomato paste and cook 1 minute. Add the tomatoes with their juice, cover and cook on a low simmer for about 5 minutes.

Add the quinoa and hot water to the saucepan, season with salt and pepper, bring to the boil, then reduce the heat, cover and simmer for about 15 minutes. Stir in the spinach and cook for a further 3–5 minutes.

Serve immediately, with some shaved parmesan cheese if using.

Broccoli and Cauliflower Panagrattato

Serves 4–6

This is an Italian way of preparing broccoli and cauliflower. *Panagrattato* means 'grated bread'—in other words, breadcrumbs. I have used quinoa flakes instead for a delicious dish that you can eat on its own or as a side dish.

500g (1lb 2oz) cauliflower
500g (1lb 2oz) broccoli
6 tbsp extra virgin olive oil, plus
    extra for serving
6 cloves garlic, sliced
4 shallots or spring onions
    (scallions), sliced
1 tsp chilli flakes
1 cup quinoa flakes
salt and freshly ground black pepper
    to taste
juice of 1 lemon

Cut the cauliflower and broccoli into florets and cook in boiling salted water until just tender but still quite crisp. Do not overcook. Drain but keep some of the cooking water.

Heat the olive oil in a large frying pan and cook the garlic, shallots and chilli for 2–4 minutes until soft and just starting to change colour. Stir the quinoa flakes into the garlic and shallots and cook for 2–3 minutes until the quinoa starts to toast. Add a little extra oil if the mixture seems dry—you want the flakes to cook and take on some colour.

Add the cooked vegetables and a little of their cooking water; toss well to combine. Season with salt, squeeze over the lemon juice and serve with an extra drizzle of extra virgin olive oil.

Spinach and Cheese Soufflé

Serves 4

The soufflé can be prepared in advance up to the stage where the egg whites are to be whisked and folded in. However, you will have to reheat the spinach mixture beforehand, otherwise the soufflé will not rise. Cover the spinach mixture with plastic wrap to stop skin from forming.

grated parmesan cheese

250g (8oz) frozen spinach leaves, thawed

1 tsp butter, plus 2½ tbsp

3 tbsp quinoa flour

1 cup hot milk

a pinch of nutmeg

4 extra-large egg yolks

90g (3oz) grated sharp or vintage cheddar cheese

30g (1oz) grated parmesan cheese

salt and pepper

5 extra-large egg whites

a pinch salt

a pinch cream of tartar

Preheat the oven to 190ºC (375ºF). Butter 4 x 1-cup capacity ramekins, then sprinkle liberally with grated parmesan cheese.

Place the spinach in a fine sieve and press with the back of a spoon to remove all moisture. Melt 1 tsp of butter in a small frying pan, add the spinach and cook on low heat for 2–3 minutes, stirring occasionally, to allow any excess moisture to evaporate. Remove from the heat.

Melt 2½ tbsp butter in a saucepan, stir in the flour to form a roux and cook for about 30 seconds, stirring constantly. Gradually stir in the milk and nutmeg and continue cooking, stirring constantly, until thickened. Remove from the heat and add the egg yolks one at a time, mixing well, then stir in the cheeses. Keep stirring until the cheese has melted then season with salt and pepper. Using a spatula, gently fold in the spinach.

Whisk the egg whites with the salt and cream of tartar until stiff and soft peaks form. Fold two large spoonfuls of egg whites into the spinach mixture to loosen it, then fold in the remaining egg whites using a metal spoon. Spoon the mixture into the ramekins. Separate the soufflé mixture from the rim of the dishes by running your finger along the edge—this will help it rise more evenly.

Place the ramekins on the middle shelf of the heated oven and bake for 25 minutes until well risen and just set. Serve immediately.

Spinach, Mushroom and Chickpea Curry

Serves 4

This is one of our favourite vegetarian family meals.

3 tbsp olive oil

1 cinnamon stick

1 tbsp cumin seeds

1 tbsp ground turmeric

1 tbsp ground coriander

1 tbsp ground cumin

2 red onion, chopped

2 long green chillies, seeded and
  chopped

350g (12½oz) mushrooms, sliced

4 cloves garlic, chopped

1 x 400g (14oz) can diced tomatoes

¾ cup quinoa grain, rinsed and
  drained

1½ cups hot water

2 x 400 (14oz) cans chickpeas,
  drained

salt to taste

150g (5oz) baby spinach leaves

½ cup coriander (cilantro)

lime juice to taste

Greek yoghurt for serving

Heat the olive oil in a large saucepan, stir in the cinnamon and cumin seeds and cook a few seconds until fragrant. Stir in turmeric, coriander and cumin and cook a few seconds more to release their flavours. Add a little more oil if needed.

Add the onion and chillies and cook until the onion is soft. Stir in the mushrooms and garlic and cook for 3–4 minutes until the mushrooms soften and collapse. Add the tomatoes, stir well and bring up to a light boil. Stir in the quinoa and water, cover and simmer on low heat for 10 minutes.

Add the chickpeas, season with salt, cover and simmer for another 5–10 minutes until the quinoa is cooked and tender. Stir in the spinach and coriander and cook until the spinach has wilted. Serve with a squeeze of lime juice and a dollop of yoghurt.

Ratatouille

Serves 4

This is one of those dishes that is a meal on its own and you can add or substitute the vegetables above with whatever other vegetables you prefer.

1 large eggplant (aubergine)

4 tbsp extra virgin olive oil

1 large brown onion, chopped

2 medium zucchini (courgettes), diced

1 large red capsicum (pepper), seeded and chopped

4 cloves garlic, finely chopped

1 x 400g (14oz) can diced tomatoes

salt and freshly ground black pepper

¾ cup quinoa grain, rinsed and drained

1 cup hot water

a small handful chopped flatleaf parsley (optional)

Preheat the oven to 170°C (325°F) and line a baking tray with baking paper.

Cut the eggplant into thick slices lengthways and cube. Drizzle and coat with 2 tbsp olive oil, place on the baking tray and bake in the heated oven for about 20 minutes, turning over once, until browned. Remove from the oven and set aside.

Meanwhile, heat the remaining olive oil in a large saucepan and cook the onion until soft and golden. Add the zucchini and capsicum and cook for about 5 minutes, until the vegetables start to go golden. Stir in the garlic and tomatoes and season with salt and pepper. Cover and simmer for 15 minutes.

Add the quinoa to the pan with the water. Stir and simmer, covered, for 15 minutes, then add the eggplant and cook for a further 5 minutes. Stir in the parsley and serve.

Curried Lentil Pilaf

Serves 4–6

You may like to remove the curry leaves after cooking as they can be a little tough. But they give an interesting texture and flavour to the dish—you just need to chew them well.

2 medium leeks

4 tbsp olive oil

4 cloves garlic, chopped

handful of fresh curry leaves

2 tsp curry powder

1 tsp garam masala

½ tsp nigella seeds

400g (14oz) green beans

1½ cups quinoa grain, rinsed and
   drained

3 cups hot water

2 x 400g (14oz) cans brown lentils,
   rinsed and drained

3–4 red chillies, deseeded and sliced

salt to taste

lemon or lime juice to taste

Wash leeks thoroughly to remove all dirt and grit and slice finely.

Heat the oil in a large saucepan or frying pan and cook the leeks until soft. Add the garlic and curry leaves and cook for about 1 minute. Stir in the curry powder, garam masala and nigella seeds and cook until fragrant, about 30 seconds.

Top and tail the beans, then slice them into two or three pieces and add to the pan. Cook for 1–2 minutes on low heat.

Add the quinoa to the pan with the water, lentils and chillies. Season with salt, stir well and then bring to the boil. Reduce the heat and simmer, covered, for 10 minutes, stirring occasionally. Switch off the heat and allow to rest for 5–10 minutes. Serve with a squeeze of lemon or lime juice.

White Cheese Sauce

**Makes: just over 2
cups**

You can make this sauce using full cream, light or soy milk. The quantities are the same.

3 tbsp butter
4 tbsp quinoa flour
2 cups milk
1 cup grated tasty cheese
salt and pepper

Melt butter in a saucepan, stir in the flour and cook for a few seconds until the butter and flour are well incorporated and a roux has formed. Pour in the milk a little at a time and whisk until free of lumps. Continue stirring until the sauce bubbles and thickens. Add the cheese and stir until it has melted and the sauce is thick and velvety smooth. Season to taste.

VARIATIONS
Curry sauce: Add 1 tsp curry powder with the flour.

Parsley sauce: Leave out the cheese and stir in ½ cup chopped parsley at the end, then stand for about 2 minutes before serving.

Plain white sauce: Leave out the cheese.

MEAT

Beef Lasagne

Serves 4–6

You can make this lasagne using lasagne sheets made out of the basic pasta dough recipe found in the Breads and Pasta chapter of this book.

1½ cups quinoa grain, rinsed and
    drained
3 cups water
1 tbsp olive oil

MINCE SAUCE

2 tbsp olive oil
1 large brown onion, finely chopped
500g (1lb 2oz) beef mince
3 cloves garlic, finely chopped
3 tbsp tomato paste
1 tsp dried oregano
1 x 400g (14oz) can diced tomatoes,
    with juice
salt and freshly ground black pepper
2 cups water

CHEESE SAUCE

4 tbsp butter
6 tbsp quinoa flour
3½ cups milk
¾ cup grated tasty cheese
¼ cup grated parmesan cheese

Preheat the oven to 185°C (360°F). Place the quinoa and water in a pan Bring to boil, reduce heat, cover and simmer for 10 minutes.

For the mince sauce, heat oil, add onion and sauté until golden. Add the mince and cook until it browns. Stir in the garlic, cook for 1 minute, then add tomato paste and cook for 1–2 minutes. Add oregano, tomatoes with juice, salt and pepper and water. Bring to the boil, then reduce the heat, cover with the lid slightly ajar, and simmer for 30–35 minutes until cooked and thick but not dry.

For the sauce, melt butter, stir in flour and cook a few seconds until the butter and flour are well incorporated and a roux is formed. Slowly pour in the milk and whisk continuously until the sauce thickens and starts to bubble. Stir in the cheese. Check for saltiness before seasoning.

Place the quinoa in a large bowl, stir through the olive oil and season.

Spread a thin layer of tcheese sauce on the bottom of a baking dish, add a third of the quinoa; flatten and top with a thin layer of cheese sauce and half the mince sauce. Repeat the layering, ending with quinoa and sauce. Sprinkle with extra parmesan cheese and bake for 30–40 minutes, until golden brown. Allow to stand for at least 30 minutes before serving.

Moroccan Beef Tagine with Cardamom Quinoa

Serves 4

4 tbsp olive oil

750g (1lb 10oz) chuck beef steak, cubed

1 leek, washed and sliced

3 cloves garlic, finely chopped

1 tbsp grated fresh ginger

1½ tsp ground cumin

1 tsp ground turmeric

2 tsp ground paprika

¼ tsp cinnamon

zest of 1 lemon

1 x 400g (14oz) can diced tomatoes, with juice

1½–2 cups water

½ bunch coriander (cilantro)

juice of ½–1 lemon

salt and freshly ground black pepper

Heat the olive oil in a large saucepan and brown the meat all over. It is best to do this in batches—if the pan is overcrowded, the beef won't brown. Set the meat aside.

Add the leeks to the pan and cook until soft, then stir in the garlic and ginger. Stir in the spices and lemon zest and add tomatoes and juice, water and the finely chopped stalks and root of the coriander (reserving the leaves for later). Cover and simmer gently for about 90 minutes, until the meat is really tender. Add more water during cooking if necessary.

Stir in the coriander leaves and lemon juice, adjust the seasoning and serve on a bed of cardamom quinoa.

CARDAMOM QUINOA

1½ cups quinoa grain, rinsed and drained

3 cups water

½ tsp ground turmeric

4–5 cardamom pods, cracked

salt

Place all the ingredients in a saucepan. Bring to the boil, then reduce the heat, cover and simmer for 10 minutes until all the water is absorbed.

Individual Eggplant Moussaka

Serves 2–4

With a Greek heritage, is it any wonder that moussaka is one of my favourite meals? These individual servings are great for a dinner party or serve half as an entrée. Lamb mince can be substituted for the beef. Serve with a Greek salad.

2 large eggplants (aubergines)
extra virgin olive oil
1–2 tbsp olive oil
450g (1lb) beef mince
1 onion, finely chopped
2 cloves garlic, finely chopped
2 tbsp tomato paste
1x 400g (14oz) can diced tomatoes
1 tsp ground cinnamon
1 cup water, plus ¾ cup
salt and pepper to taste
½ cup quinoa grain, rinsed and
    drained

WHITE SAUCE
1 tbsp butter
1 tbsp quinoa flour
1 cup milk
1 tsp grated parmesan cheese

Preheat the oven to 170°C (340°F). Cut the eggplants in half lengthways, keeping the stalk intact. Trim a fine slice off the bottom of each half. Scoop out and reserve as much pulp as possible, leaving a firm but not too thick shell. Brush all over with extra virgin olive oil and place on a lined baking tray. Bake for about 20 minutes, until tender.

Heat 1–2 tbsp olive oil in a large frying pan and brown the mince, then add the onion and garlic and cook 2–4 minutes, until the onion is soft. Roughly chop the reserved eggplant pulp and stir it into the mince. Add the tomato paste and cook for 1–2 minutes, then add the tomatoes, cinnamon, water, salt and pepper, and simmer for 10 minutes.

Stir in the quinoa and extra water and simmer, covered, on low heat for another 15–20 minutes, stirring occasionally. Cool slightly.

For the sauce, melt the butter in a saucepan and stir in the flour. Slowly pour in the milk, stirring until it starts to bubble. Stir in cheese and pepper and cook until the sauce thickens.

Fill each eggplant with mince, cover with sauce and sprinkle with cinnamon and parmesan. Bake for 20–30 minutes until golden.

Crumbed Lamb Cutlets with Garlic, Lemon and Oregano

Serves 4–6

12 lamb cutlets

1 cup quinoa flakes

2–3 cloves garlic, finely grated

zest of 1 lemon

2 tsp dried oregano leaves

salt and freshly ground black pepper

80g (3oz) quinoa flour

2 eggs, lightly beaten

olive oil for shallow-frying

squeeze of lemon juice

Trim the cutlets of any excess fat and lightly pound with a mallet to flatten.

Combine the quinoa flakes with the garlic, lemon zest, oregano, salt and pepper; set aside.

Lightly dust each cutlet with some flour, dip in the beaten egg, then press into the quinoa flake mixture and coat well.

Heat the oil in a large frying pan until hot and gently shallow-fry the cutlets on a medium heat until golden, about 2–3 minutes each side. Serve hot with a squeeze of lemon juice.

Mushroom Meatballs

Makes 10–12 walnut-sized meatballs

You can make these in whatever size you like. They are great cold and in sandwiches.

½ cup red quinoa grain, rinsed and
  drained
1 cup water
300g (10½oz) mushrooms
500g (1lb 2oz) beef mince
1 large onion, grated
3 cloves garlic, grated
4 tbsp chopped flatleaf parsley
2 tsp dried oregano leaves
2 eggs
salt and pepper to taste
½ cup quinoa flour
olive oil for frying

Place the quinoa in a small saucepan. Bring to the boil, then reduce the heat, cover and simmer for 10 minutes until all the water is absorbed. Remove from the heat and set aside.

Wipe the mushrooms lightly with a damp cloth and finely chop. Put them in a large mixing bowl with the quinoa and all the other ingredients except for quinoa flour and oil and mix well.

Shape spoonfuls of the mixture into round balls the size of a large walnut, lightly dust with flour and shallow-fry in hot oil until cooked.

Lamb with Pomegranate, Mint and Nuts

Serves 4

1 cup quinoa grain, rinsed and
  drained
2 cups water
750g (1lb 10oz) lamb fillets
2 tbsp olive oil, plus 1 tsp for the
  lamb
60g (2oz) skinless almond kernels
45g (1½oz) pine nuts
1 cup golden raisins or sultanas
60g (2oz) pistachio nuts
salt and pepper to taste
1 large pomegranate
¾ cup chopped mint
salt and freshly ground black pepper
  to taste

Place the quinoa and water in a small pan. Bring to the boil, then reduce the heat and simmer, covered, for 10 minutes until all the water is absorbed. Remove from the heat and set aside.

Heat a griddle pan or frying pan until hot. Rub the lamb fillets on both sides with a little olive oil and season with salt and pepper. Place in the hot pan, sear well on both sides and cook to your liking; about 3–4 minutes on each side if you want the meat pink. Place on a plate, cover tightly with foil to keep warm and allow to rest.

Heat 2 tablespoons of olive oil in a large frying pan, add the almonds and gently toast until they start to change colour. Add the pine nuts and sultanas and cook for another 1–2 minutes. Keep a close eye on them as the nuts and sultanas tend to colour quickly.

Stir in the cooked quinoa and pistachio nuts and mix well. Slice the lamb into thin slices and add to the pan with any meat juices left on the plate.

Cut the pomegranate in half and, with the back of a wooden spoon, bash the fruit straight out of both halves and into the pan. Give a little squeeze to release any juice. Stir in the mint, check the seasoning and serve.

Lamb with Garlic, Cumin and Peas

Serves 4

This is great served with some finely sliced red chillies and lemon wedges. A dollop of thick Greek yoghurt is very nice with it also. If you are sensitive to gluten/wheat, use a wheat-free tamari soy sauce.

2 tbsp olive oil

2 medium onions

500g (1lb 2oz) minced lamb

4 cloves garlic, chopped

1 tsp cumin seeds

1 heaped tbsp ground cumin

1 cup quinoa grain, rinsed and
    drained

1 tbsp soy sauce

chilli powder to taste

salt

2 cups hot water

1 cup frozen peas

red chillies for serving

lemon wedges for serving

Heat the olive oil in a large deep frying pan. Cut onions in half and thinly slice. Add to the pan and cook until soft and golden. Add the mince and cook until well browned. Stir in the garlic, cumin seeds and ground cumin and cook for 1–2 minutes, until fragrant. Add the quinoa, soy sauce, chilli powder, salt and water. Stir, cover and simmer on low heat for 10–15 minutes, until the quinoa is almost cooked. Add a little extra water if the mixture is too dry. Stir in the frozen peas and cook for another 10 minutes.

Bacon Meat Loaf

Serves 6

This is a family favourite among the men in my family and it goes such a long way. Leftover meat loaf sandwiches are just the best. If you are sensitive to gluten/wheat, omit the Worcestershire sauce.

750g (1lb 10oz) minced beef
1 medium onion, coarsely grated
1 medium carrot, coarsely grated
3 cloves garlic, finely grated
⅔ cup frozen peas, thawed
¾ cup quinoa flakes
2 tsp dried oregano leaves
¼ cup tomato sauce/ketchup
1 tbsp Worcestershire sauce
2 eggs
3 tbsp chopped flatleaf parsley
salt and freshly ground black pepper
5–6 rashers of bacon

Preheat the oven to 175°C (340°F).

Place the mince in a large bowl with all the other ingredients except for the bacon and mix thoroughly.

Lightly oil a large loaf tin and line with the bacon slices—place them, side by side, across the bottom of the tin, letting them overhang the sides of the tin. Spoon the meatloaf mixture on top of the bacon and level the top. Fold the overhanging bacon rashers over the meatloaf to enclose.

Bake in the oven for about 1–1½ hours, until cooked and browned. If the top is browning too quickly cover with foil. Rest for 10–15 minutes before slicing.

Pea and Ham Mint Pie

Serves 6

This reheats beautifully and is lovely for a luncheon with a crisp green salad.

½ cup quinoa grain, rinsed and
 drained
1 cup water
4 large eggs
2 cups milk
1 heaped tbsp prepared English
 mustard
150g (5oz) diced ham
4 shallots (eschalot), thinly sliced
1 cup grated tasty cheese
salt and freshly ground black pepper
1 heaped tbsp chopped mint
2 cups frozen peas, thawed

Preheat the oven to 160°C (315°F). Lightly butter a round tart dish.

Place the quinoa in a small saucepan with the water. Bring to the boil, then reduce the heat, cover and simmer for 10 minutes until all the water is absorbed. Remove from heat and cool.

Whisk together the eggs, milk and mustard. Fold in the quinoa and all other ingredients until thoroughly combined.

Pour the mixture into the prepared tart dish and bake for about 45–50 minutes, until the filling is set and the top is golden.

Chorizo Sausage with Peas and Tomatoes

Serves 4

You can substitute prawns or strips of chicken breast for the chorizo. If using chicken, cook it almost completely at the beginning. Prawns can be added at the last but vary the cooking time accordingly.

3 chorizo sausages

2 tbsp olive oil

1 large onion, finely chopped

3 large cloves garlic, finely chopped

1 tsp sweet paprika

1 x 400g (14oz) can cherry tomatoes, undrained

2 cups quinoa grain, rinsed and drained

3 cups hot water

salt and pepper

2 cups frozen peas

3 tbsp chopped flatleaf parsley

2 tbsp chopped chives

Cut the chorizo into quarters lengthways, then into pieces. Heat the oil in a large deep frying pan and cook the chorizo until golden, then remove from the pan.

Add the onion and sauté until soft, adding a little extra oil if needed. Stir in the garlic and cook until fragrant, then add the paprika, cherry tomatoes, quinoa and water. Season to taste, cover and simmer for 10 minutes. Stir in the peas, parsley, chives and chorizo and simmer, covered, for a further 8–10 minutes.

POULTRY

Roast Chicken with a Spicy Garlic Stuffing

Serves 4

½ cup quinoa grain, rinsed and
    drained
1 cup water
1 chicken, about 2kg (4lb 8oz)
2 tbsp olive oil
1 medium onion, finely chopped
2 rashers of bacon, rind removed,
    chopped
4 cloves garlic, finely chopped
3 shallots (eschalots) or spring
    onions (scallions), sliced
1½ tsp ground cumin
1 tsp ground turmeric
1 tsp curry powder
1 tsp chilli flakes
4 tbsp water
olive oil (extra)
juice of 1 lemon
salt and freshly ground black pepper

Preheat the oven to 175ºC (340ºF).

Place the quinoa in a small saucepan with the water. Bring to the boil, then reduce the heat, cover and simmer for 10 minutes until all the water is absorbed. Remove from the heat.

Remove any excess fat from the chicken, rinse under cold water and thoroughly pat dry with kitchen paper. Set aside.

Heat the olive oil in a large frying pan, add the onion and bacon and cook until the onion is soft and bacon crispy. Add the garlic and shallots and cook for 1 minute. Stir in the cumin, turmeric, curry powder and chilli and cook until fragrant, then stir in the cooked quinoa. If the mixture seems too dry, add a little water.

Sprinkle the inside of the chicken cavity with a little of the lemon juice, then fill it with the quinoa stuffing mixture. Secure the opening with a metal skewer.

Place the chicken on a baking tray, rub with olive oil all over, sprinkle with the remaining lemon juice and season to taste. Roast for 1½–1¾ hours, until the chicken is cooked and golden all over.

Chicken Rissoles

Makes about 15

These rissoles, which can be eaten hot or cold, are great to take on picnics. You can use chicken thigh or breast mince or even substitute with pork mince if you prefer.

½ cup quinoa grain, rinsed and
    drained
1 cup water
1 kg (2lb 3oz) chicken mince
1 large onion, finely chopped
3 cloves garlic, finely chopped
1½ tbsp Dijon mustard
3 shallots or spring onions
    (scallions), thinly sliced
⅓ cup chopped flatleaf parsley
⅓ cup chopped coriander (cilantro)
1 red chilli, finely chopped
2 eggs
salt and freshly ground black pepper
olive oil for shallow-frying

Place the quinoa in a small saucepan with the water. Bring to the boil, then reduce the heat, cover and simmer for 10 minutes. Remove from the heat and cool slightly.

Place the cooled quinoa in a large bowl with all other ingredients except for oil and mix thoroughly.

Take small handfuls of the mixture and shape into rounds about 3cm (1in) thick. Heat the oil in a frying pan and shallow-fry the rissoles until cooked and golden.

Roast Chicken with Bacon, Mustard and Herb Stuffing

Serves 4–6

1 chicken, about 2kg (4lb 8oz)

1 tbsp olive oil

juice of 1 lemon

1 tsp dried oregano leaves

salt and pepper

STUFFING

1 tbsp olive oil

1 small onion, finely chopped

3 bacon rashers, rind removed,
  chopped

¾ cup quinoa flakes

1 tbsp prepared English mustard

2 tbsp chopped flatleaf parsley

2 tbsp chopped chives

1 tsp fresh thyme leaves

1 tsp dried oregano leaves

zest of 1 lemon

1 egg

freshly ground black pepper

Preheat the oven to 170°C (340°F).

To prepare the stuffing, heat the oil in a small frying pan and brown the onion and bacon. Turn into a bowl and add all the other stuffing ingredients. Mix well until thoroughly combined.

Remove any excess fat from the chicken, rinse under cold water and thoroughly pat dry with kitchen paper. Place in a roasting dish. Spoon the stuffing mixture into the chicken cavity and secure the opening with a metal skewer. Rub the skin with olive oil, pour over the lemon juice, sprinkle with oregano and season with salt and pepper. Roast for about 1½–1¾ hours, until the chicken is cooked and golden.

You can add your favourite vegetables to the roasting dish around the chicken if you wish. Cover the chicken with foil if it starts to brown too quickly.

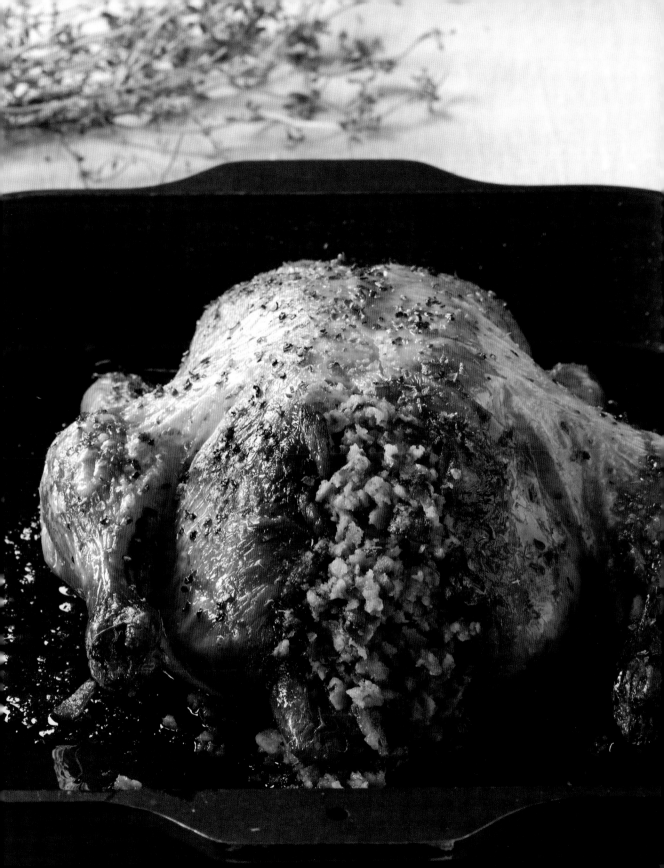

Chicken Fillets with Pancetta, Olives and Sun-dried Tomatoes

Serves 4

This is a great dinner-party dish, especially if you or any of your guests are wheat- or gluten-intolerant and you want to make something special which can be enjoyed by everyone.

4 chicken breast fillets

½ cup quinoa flakes

4 slices pancetta, chopped

8 kalamata olives, chopped

90g (3oz) sun- or semi-dried
  tomatoes, chopped

1 tbsp grated parmesan cheese
  (optional)

1 tsp dried oregano leaves

1 shallot or spring onion (scallion),
  finely sliced

1 tbsp extra virgin olive oil

1 tsp balsamic vinegar

2 tbsp water

salt and freshly ground black pepper

parsley, chopped, for garnish

SAUCE

400g (14oz) can diced tomatoes

¼ cup water

1 tsp dried oregano leaves

salt and pepper

Preheat the oven to 175ºC (340ºF).

Cut a deep pocket into the chicken fillets, taking care not to cut right through.

Combine the quinoa flakes with the pancetta, olives, tomatoes, cheese, oregano, shallots, olive oil, vinegar and water. Add salt and pepper to taste, but season carefully as the pancetta and olives and parmesan can be quite salty.

Spoon the filling into the pockets in the chicken and smooth the top part of the fillet over the filling to enclose.

Mix all the sauce ingredients together and pour into a baking dish. Place the fillets on top, drizzle with extra virgin olive oil and bake for 25–30 minutes, until the chicken is cooked. Add a little extra water to the sauce if necessary during cooking.

Serve with the sauce spooned over the chicken and garnished with parsley.

Spicy Chicken, Apricot and Almond Tagine

Serves 4

1 tsp ground paprika

1 tsp ground ginger

1 tsp ground cumin

chilli powder to taste

2 chicken breast fillets, skinned and
   halved

60g (2oz) flaked almonds

2 tbsp olive oil

4 shallots or spring onions
   (scallions), sliced

2 cloves garlic, sliced finely

1 cup quinoa grain, rinsed and
   drained

2 cups chicken stock

125g (4oz) dried apricots, finely
   sliced

2 tbsp apricot jam

salt and freshly ground black pepper

$\frac{1}{3}$ cup coriander (cilantro) leaves,
   roughly chopped

Preheat the oven to 180°C (350°F). Line a baking tray with baking paper.

Mix the paprika, ginger, cumin and chilli together. Rub the spice mixture all over the chicken breasts, season with salt and place on the baking tray. Drizzle the chicken with a little olive oil, cover with foil and place in the oven. Roast for about 15–20 minutes, until the chicken is cooked. Do not overcook or it will dry out. Remove from the oven and rest, covered.

Dry-roast almonds in a small non-stick pan over low heat until golden; set aside.

Heat the oil in a large frying pan and cook the shallots and garlic for 1–2 minutes. Stir in the quinoa, stock and dried apricots and apricot jam. Season with salt and pepper, cover and simmer for 10–15 minutes until the quinoa has absorbed all the stock and is cooked.

Slice the chicken into bite-sized pieces, toss into the quinoa with the almonds and coriander leaves and any pan juices from the chicken. Heat through and serve.

Christmas Turkey with Pork and Cranberry Stuffing

Serves 10–12

You can use chicken mince in place of the pork mince.

1 tbsp butter
2 tbsp olive oil
1 large onion, finely chopped
450g (1lb) pork mince
125g (4oz) dried cranberries
1 tbsp honey
2 tbsp Dijon mustard
1½ cups quinoa flakes
1 tsp ground cinnamon
a pinch ground cloves
4 tbsp chopped flatleaf parsley
juice of ½ lemon
zest and juice of 1 orange
salt and freshly ground black pepper
2 eggs, lightly beaten
1 turkey, 5–6kg (10–12lb)
juice of 1 lemon
olive oil, extra

Preheat the oven to 200°C (400°F).

Heat the butter and oil in a large frying pan and sauté onion until soft. Add mince and cook for 3–4 minutes, stirring occasionally and breaking up lumps. Stir in the cranberries and cook for 2 minutes. Off the heat, stir in the honey, mustard and cool slightly.

Add the quinoa flakes, cinnamon, cloves, parsley, lemon juice and the orange zest and juice to the pork, season with salt and pepper and mix well. Stir in the eggs, mix well.

Clean the turkey carefully and rinse under running water and dry well. Spoon the stuffing into turkey cavity and secure with skewers. Place any leftover stuffing in neck cavity.

Place the turkey into a large roasting dish, season all over by rubbing with lemon juice, olive oil, salt and pepper. Roast in the heated oven for 30 minutes, then reduce the heat to 170°C (325°F) and roast for a further 2½–3 hours, until the turkey is cooked. Cover with foil if the turkey is browning too quickly. Baste with pan juices during cooking and add water to the pan if the juices dry out.

To check if cooked through, insert a metal skewer into thickest part, usually the thigh. If the juices run clear, the bird is cooked. Rest, covered with foil, for 20 minutes before serving.

Herb-crumbed Chicken Tenderloins

Serves 6

If you prefer, you can leave out the herbs or substitute other favourites. Either way, these are always a great hit and kids love them. They are good served with a Thai sweet chilli sauce.

1 kg (2lb 3oz) chicken breast
    tenderloins
1½ cups quinoa flakes
1 tbsp chopped thyme leaves
1 tbsp chopped chives
salt and freshly ground black pepper
¾ cup quinoa flour
2–3 eggs, lightly beaten
light olive oil for shallow-frying

Trim any fat and any bits of tendons from the tenderloins.

Combine the quinoa flakes with the herbs, salt and pepper.

Dust the tenderloins with flour, dip them in the beaten egg, then coat with the flake mixture, pressing down to make sure the tenderloins are well covered.

Heat the oil until hot and gently shallow-fry on a medium heat about 3 minutes on each side, until they are cooked through and golden brown.

Chicken Mexicana

Serves 4

Another one-pot favourite, this is a really good meal to prepare when your children have friends over for dinner.

3 tbsp olive oil

2 medium red onions, chopped

800g (28oz) chicken thigh fillets, diced

3–4 cloves garlic, chopped

1 tbsp ground paprika

1 tsp dried oregano leaves

2 tsp ground cumin

1 tsp ground chilli

1 red capsicum (pepper), deseeded and cut into chunks

1 green capsicum (pepper), deseeded and cut into chunks

1 x 400g (14oz) can diced tomatoes, with juice

salt

1 cup quinoa grain, rinsed and drained

2 x 400g (14oz) cans red kidney beans, rinsed and drained

1½ cups hot water

GARNISH

1–2 avocados

sour cream or Greek yoghurt

coriander (cilantro), chopped

Heat the olive oil in a large frying pan and sauté the onions until soft and golden. Add the chicken and cook for 3–5 minutes, until sealed all over. Stir in the garlic, paprika, oregano, cumin and chilli and cook for about 30 seconds until fragrant.

Stir in the capsicums, tomatoes and juice and season with salt. Reduce the heat, cover and simmer for 10 minutes. Add the quinoa to the pan with the red kidney beans and water. Stir well, bring back to a simmer, cover and cook for about 15 minutes, stirring occasionally until the quinoa and chicken are cooked.

Serve with slices of avocado, a dollop of sour cream or plain yoghurt and chopped coriander leaves.

Chicken and Preserved Lemon Tagine with Coconut Quinoa

Serves 4

1 kg (2lb 3oz) chicken thigh fillets
1½ tsp ground coriander
1 tsp ground turmeric
1 tsp ground ginger
1 tsp ground cumin
salt and freshly ground black pepper
1 large onion, halved and thinly
  sliced
1 preserved lemon
4 cloves garlic, chopped
½ cup stuffed green olives
a generous pinch of saffron
olive oil
½ cup water

Cut the chicken thigh fillets in half and place in a large plastic bag. Mix the coriander, turmeric, ginger, cumin, salt and pepper together and sprinkle over the chicken, then give the bag a really good shake to coat the chicken with the spices.

Place half the onion slices in the bottom of a large frying pan which has a tight fitting lid, place the chicken pieces on top in a single layer and then cover with the remaining onion slices.

Remove and discard the pulp from the preserved lemon, chop the rind into small pieces and then scatter them over chicken, along with the garlic and olives,

Sprinkle with saffron and a good drizzle of olive oil. Add the water, swirl the pan and cover tightly with lid. Bring to the boil, then reduce heat and simmer on low heat for 45–50 minutes, until the chicken is cooked and the onions are soft. Serve with coconut quinoa.

COCONUT QUINOA

1½ cups quinoa grain, rinsed and
  drained
1½ cups coconut milk
1½ cups hot water
lemon zest
coriander (cilantro), chopped

Place the quinoa in a medium-sized saucepan with the coconut milk and water. Bring to the boil, cover and simmer on low heat for 10–15 minutes, until all the liquid has been absorbed. Lightly stir in the lemon zest and coriander with a fork before serving with the chicken.

Quail with Rocket, Garlic and Pine Nut Stuffing

Serves 4

30g (1oz) pine nuts

2 tbsp olive oil

2 shallots (eschalots), finely chopped

4 shallots or spring onions (scallions), finely sliced

3 large cloves garlic, finely chopped

150g (5oz) baby rocket, roughly chopped

salt and freshly ground black pepper

2 tsp balsamic vinegar

½ cup quinoa flakes

1 egg

8 quails

olive oil

juice of 1 lemon

½ cup white wine

1 tsp chopped thyme leaves

1 tsp chopped rosemary leaves

ground paprika

Preheat the oven to 185°C (360°F).

Lightly dry-roast the pine nuts in a small non-stick frying pan. Set aside to cool.

Heat the olive oil in a frying pan and sauté the eschalots and spring onions until golden. Stir in the garlic and cook for another 30 seconds. Add the rocket, salt and pepper, stir, cover and cook on medium heat for about 2–3 minutes until the rocket wilts. Cool slightly, then mix in the balsamic vinegar, roasted pine nuts, quinoa flakes and egg.

Prepare the quails: remove any feathers, rinse under running water and pat dry. Fill each quail with the stuffing mixture and tie the bottom of the drumsticks together with kitchen string.

Place the quails into a roasting dish, rub with olive oil and pour over the lemon juice and wine. Sprinkle with thyme, rosemary and paprika and season with salt and pepper. Cover with foil and roast for 15 minutes, then remove the foil and roast for another 20–30 minutes, until the quails are golden and cooked, basting occasionally with the pan juices. Add water to the pan if the liquid dries out.

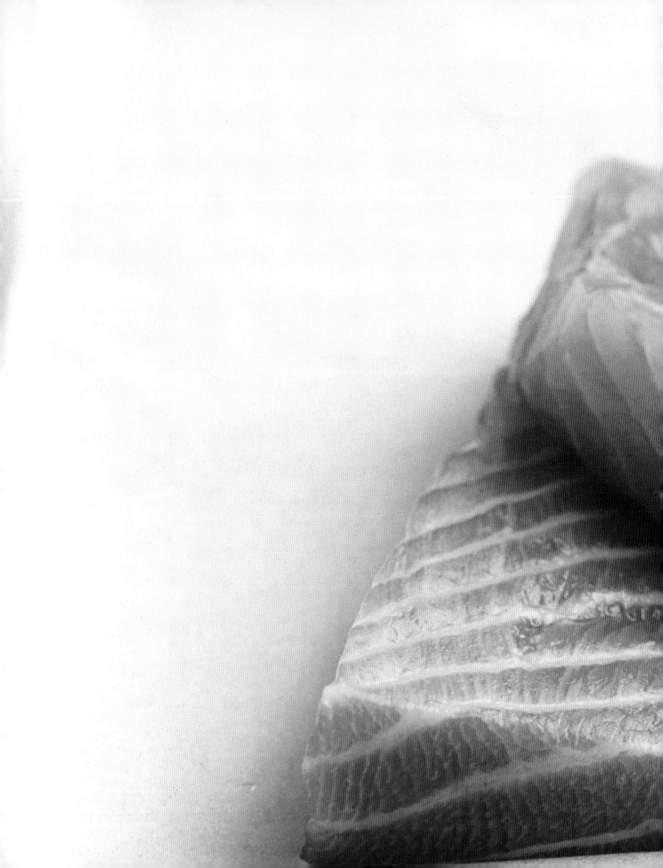

SEAFOOD

Tuna with Tomatoes and Olives

Serves 4–6

I love this dish as I am a huge fan of tuna and best of all, it is a one-pot dish.

3 tbsp extra virgin olive oil, plus
    extra for serving
1 large onion, finely chopped
3 cloves garlic, finely chopped
1 generous tbsp tomato paste
1 x 400g (14oz) can diced tomatoes,
    with juice
½ cup roughly chopped flatleaf
    parsley, plus extra for serving
salt and freshly ground black pepper
2 x 425g (15oz) cans tuna in spring
    water, drained
1 cup uncooked quinoa grain
¾–1 cup pitted black olives
1 cup water
lemon wedges

Heat the olive oil in a large saucepan and sauté the onion until soft and golden. Stir in the garlic and cook until fragrant, about 30 seconds, then stir in the tomato paste and cook for about 1 minute more.

Stir in the tomatoes with their juice, parsley, salt and pepper and cook on low heat for about 10 minutes. Add the tuna and cook for another 5 minutes. Add the quinoa with the olives and water. Stir well, bring to the boil, reduce heat, cover and simmer for 10–15 minutes, until the quinoa is cooked and all the liquid has been absorbed.

Stir in the extra parsley and drizzle with some extra virgin olive oil before serving with lemon wedges.

Salmon Croquettes

Makes 16

This is an inexpensive and delicious meal and very popular with children. Try making little mini ones for very young children.

1 x 415g (14½oz) can red salmon
2 large potatoes, cooked, mashed
   and cooled
1 large onion, grated
3 tbsp chopped flatleaf parsley
salt and freshly ground black pepper
2 large eggs
3 tbsp quinoa flour
1 cup quinoa flakes
vegetable or olive oil for frying

Drain the salmon well, remove all the bones and flake.

Place the salmon in a large bowl with the mashed potato, onion, parsley, salt, pepper, eggs and flour. Gently mix to thoroughly combine. The mixture should be quite wet.

With wet hands, take spoonfuls of the mixture and form into long cylinder shapes about 8cm (3½in) long.

Roll each croquette in the quinoa flakes. Heat the oil in a frying pan and shallow-fry the croquettes on medium to low heat until golden, about 2–3 minutes on each side. Keep an eye on them so they don't brown too quickly. It is best not to overcrowd the pan.

Spanish-style Mussels

Serves 4

3 tbsp extra virgin olive oil

1 medium red onion, finely chopped

6 shallots or spring onions
(scallions), sliced

1 green capsicum (pepper), seeded
and sliced

1 red capsicum (pepper), seeded and
sliced

4–5 cloves garlic, finely chopped

½ cup white wine

a good pinch of saffron threads

2 x 400g (14oz) cans diced tomatoes

½–1 tsp dried chilli flakes

1kg (2.2lb) mussels

1 cup quinoa grain, rinsed and
drained

¾ cup hot water

salt and pepper

1 cup green stuffed olives

a handful chopped flatleaf parsley

lemon wedges for serving

Heat the olive oil in a large frying pan and sauté the onion, shallots and capsicums until soft, then stir in the garlic and cook for 30 seconds. Pour in the wine, deglaze the pan and cook for 1–2 minutes. Add the saffron, tomatoes and chilli, stir and cook on low heat, covered, for about 5–7 minutes until the sauce thickens.

Meanwhile, prepare the mussels by pulling out the beards and scraping off any barnacles; rinse well. Discard any that are open.

Add the quinoa to the pan with the water, season with salt and pepper, stir, and simmer, covered, for about 7 minutes, stirring occasionally. Watch it to make sure it does not dry out—avoid adding any more liquid because the mussels will release a lot of their own liquor. Add the mussels, cover and cook for another 8–10 minutes, stirring occasionally until the quinoa is cooked and the mussels are open.

Stir in the olives and parsley and serve with lemon wedges.

Mustard-crusted Salmon with Dill and Lemon

Serves 4

A delicious and different way to serve salmon. It is lovely for a luncheon served with a big salad.

4 salmon fillets, about 200g (7oz)
   each
2 tbsp Dijon mustard
3 tbsp chopped dill
2 tbsp chopped flatleaf parsley
1 large clove garlic, grated
zest of 1 lemon
2–3 tbsp lemon juice
1 shallot (eschalot) or spring onion
   (scallion), finely sliced including
   the greens
1 tbsp olive oil
1 cup quinoa flakes
salt and freshly ground black pepper
lemon juice to serve
sprigs of dill to serve

Preheat the oven to 180°C (350°F).

Trim the salmon fillets to an even shape and place, skin side down, on a roasting tray that has been lined with baking paper.

Place the mustard in a bowl with the dill, parsley, garlic, lemon zest, juice, spring onion and olive oil. Mix thoroughly to combine. Mix in the quinoa flakes, salt and pepper. Use your hands to mix and squeeze the mixture together so it holds.

Divide the mixture into four and spread evenly on top of each fillet. Drizzle with extra virgin olive oil and roast for 15–20 minutes until the topping is golden and the salmon is cooked.

Serve with a squeeze of lemon juice and sprigs of dill.

Prawn 'Risotto'

Serves 4

You may hear and read that the Italians never ever sprinkle parmesan cheese on any seafood pasta or risotto dish. This is a very individual thing—in my family we always have, and my dear grandmother would be absolutely horrified if she thought we were doing it any differently.

3 tbsp olive oil

1 onion, finely chopped

3 shallots or spring onions (scallions), sliced

2 large cloves garlic, finely chopped

1 cup quinoa grain, rinsed and drained

½ cup white wine

1 x 400g (14oz) can diced tomatoes

salt and freshly ground black pepper

2 cups hot water

500g (1lb 2oz) peeled and deveined prawns

½ cup frozen peas

a knob of butter

2 tbsp chopped flatleaf parsley

grated parmesan (optional)

Heat the olive oil in a large saucepan and cook the onions and shallots on medium heat for about 5 minutes until soft. Stir in the garlic. Add the quinoa to the pan and stir. Add the wine and cook until the alcohol has evaporated and all the liquid has been absorbed. Stir in the tomatoes, salt, pepper and hot water.

Cover and cook on a low simmer for 10 minutes, stirring occasionally. Add the prawns and peas and simmer, covered, for another 10–12 minutes until the prawns are cooked. Stir in a good knob of butter, parsley and parmesan cheese, if using, and serve immediately.

Whole Snapper with a Mushroom and Leek Stuffing

Serves 4

This is a great dish for a dinner party and looks good brought to the table on a platter.

½ cup quinoa grain, rinsed and
    drained

1 cup water

2 tbsp olive oil

1 leek, washed and finely sliced

250g (8oz) mushrooms, sliced

salt and freshly ground black pepper

2 large cloves garlic, finely chopped

2 tbsp chopped flatleaf parsley

1 tsp dried oregano leaves

1 x 1.5kg (3lb) whole snapper, scaled
    and cleaned

juice of 1 lemon

extra virgin olive oil

1 large tomato, sliced

1 red onion, sliced

2 shallots (eschalots) or spring
    onions (scallions), chopped

1 tbsp chopped flatleaf parsley

Preheat the oven to 185°C (360°F).

Place the quinoa in a small saucepan with the water. Bring to the boil, then reduce the heat, cover and simmer for 10 minutes until all the water is absorbed. Remove from the heat.

Heat the olive oil in a frying pan and sauté the leek until soft. Add the mushrooms, season with salt and pepper and cook until the mushrooms are soft. Stir in the garlic, then the parsley and oregano. Remove the pan from the heat, mix in the cooked quinoa and adjust the seasoning.

Place the fish on a large ovenproof dish that has been lined with baking paper. Sprinkle the cavity of the fish with some lemon juice and fill it with the stuffing mixture. Pour the remaining lemon juice over the fish and drizzle with extra virgin olive oil.

Place in the oven and bake for 15 minutes. Remove from the oven and arrange alternate slices of tomato and onion over the fish and sprinkle with the shallots and parsley. Loosely cover with foil, return to the oven and continue baking for another 30 minutes or until fish is cooked. Remove foil in the last 10 minutes or so of cooking to allow the tomatoes and onion to take on some colour.

Salt and Pepper Squid

Serves 6

1kg (2lb 3oz) whole squid
2 cups quinoa flour
¾ cup cold water
2 tbsp crushed sea salt
1 tbsp white pepper
1 tbsp coarsely ground black pepper
1–2 tsp chilli flakes
vegetable oil for deep-frying
lemon wedges for serving

Either buy ready-cleaned squid hoods or whole squid and clean them yourself, in which case you will have the tentacles to cook as well.

Slice the squid hood in half so it lays flat and, with a sharp knife, lightly score the inside part of the squid (without cutting right through) diagonally to form diamond shapes, then cut into thick strips. If you are using the tentacles, cut them in half.

Mix ¾ cup of flour with the water to form a paste. Mix together the remaining flour with the salt, white and black peppers and the chilli flakes. (I suggest that you start with a lesser amount of salt and pepper, cook a couple of pieces to check and adjust your seasoning.)

Dip the squid pieces and tentacles into the batter, then into the flour mixture and deep-fry in hot oil until they curl, crisp up and turn golden brown. You may need to change the oil once during cooking. Drain on kitchen paper and serve hot with wedges of lemon.

NOTE

Clean the squid by gently pulling and separating the head from the hood. Carefully remove and discard the ink sac and fine cartilage, then gently pull away the very fine dark skin. The wings will come away with the skin. Cut off a small piece at the base of the hood to allow water to freely run through and clean out anything that may be left behind. Rinse the cleaned squid thoroughly in cold water.

To clean the heads, remove the eyes and the thick membrane that is near them, by cutting them off just above the eye area.

Ready-cleaned squid is usually frozen and can be quite tough—buying it fresh and cleaning it yourself is preferable.

Beer-battered Fish

Serves 4

Depending on what type and size of fish fillets you use, you could have some batter left over. The above ratio of flour to liquid works best for a light and crispy batter.

1kg (2lb 3oz) firm white fish fillets
2 cups quinoa flour, plus extra for dusting
about 330ml (11½fl oz) cold gluten-free beer
½ cup cold sparkling mineral water
sea salt
pepper
vegetable or light olive oil for deep frying
lemon wedges for serving

Place the flour into a large bowl and, using a whisk, mix the beer and water into the flour until you have a smooth batter. Season with salt and pepper.

Heat the oil in a frying pan or deep-fryer until the oil is medium hot—if the oil is too hot, the fish will burn very quickly without cooking properly.

Lightly dust each fish fillet with a little extra quinoa flour, then dip into the batter, shake off any excess batter and carefully slide into the hot oil. Cook for 2–3 minutes on each side, until crisp and golden. Remove from oil and drain on kitchen paper. Serve immediately with fresh lemon wedges.

SWEET
THINGS

Apple and Cinnamon Buttermilk Pancakes

Makes 8–10 pancakes

The buttermilk makes the pancakes light and fluffy. They are best eaten as soon as they are cooked—they are delicious as they are or with a drizzle of maple sugar or a light dusting of icing sugar. Make sure to use a sweet-tasting apple—it really makes a difference.

1 large egg
½ cup caster sugar
1 tsp ground cinnamon
1 tsp vanilla extract
1 cup buttermilk
1 cup quinoa flour
1 large sweet apple, unpeeled and coarsely grated (I prefer red delicious)
unsalted butter for cooking

Whisk the egg and sugar together until light, then mix in the cinnamon and vanilla. Whisk in the buttermilk until combined, then slowly mix in the flour a little at a time until you get a smooth, lump-free mixture. Fold in the grated apple.

Heat a small non-stick frying pan until hot and add a little butter. When melted, pour in small ladlefuls of pancake mixture. Swirl the pan around to form an even pancake and cook on both sides until golden. Serve immediately.

Apple and Cinnamon Crumble

Serves 4–6

This is a delicious, sweet and crispy crumble, a twist on the Apple Brown Betty. The quinoa flakes mixed with the sugar form crispy clusters that are very yummy!

6 large green granny smith apples
1 cup brown sugar, loosely packed
2 heaped tsp ground cinnamon,
　　plus ½ tsp
$\frac{1}{8}$ tsp ground nutmeg
$\frac{1}{8}$ tsp ground cloves
$\frac{1}{8}$ tsp ground allspice
1 cup quinoa flakes
125g (4oz) unsalted butter

Preheat the oven to 170ºC (325ºF).

Peel and core the apples, then cut into quarters and slice into ¾cm (½in) slices and place in a bowl.

In a separate bowl combine the sugar, 2 heaped teaspoons of cinnamon, the nutmeg, cloves, allspice and quinoa flakes.

Melt butter and pour into the sugar mixture, mix well.

Take 2 tablespoons of the sugar mixture, add ½ teaspoons of cinnamon and toss through the apples with your hands.

Place the apples into a baking dish, top with the remaining sugar mixture and bake for about 40 minutes, until the apples are soft and the crumble is crisp.

Serve warm or cold on its own or with vanilla ice cream.

Blueberry Friands

Makes 9 friands

You can substitute raspberries or blackberries for the blueberries if you prefer.

125g (4oz) almond meal

1 cup icing sugar, sifted

60g (2oz) quinoa flour

125g (4oz) unsalted butter, melted
  and cooled

½ tsp vanilla extract

4 large egg whites

250g (8oz) fresh blueberries

Preheat the oven to 170ºC (325ºF). Grease a 9-cup friand tin with butter.

Place the almond meal, icing sugar and quinoa flour in a bowl. Using a whisk, mix well, breaking up any lumps of mixture that may form. Lightly mix in the melted butter and vanilla extract.

Beat the egg whites until foamy and soft peaks form, and gently fold into the mixture.

Spoon the mixture into the prepared tin. Place 5–6 blueberries around the centre of each friand and lightly press them down into the mixture.

Bake for about 25 minutes, until lightly browned and cooked when a metal skewer comes out clean.

Apple and Orange Breakfast Porridge

Serves 4

You can prepare this breakfast 'porridge' and keep it in the refrigerator—to re-heat and use as required (it keeps for 4–5 days).

3 cups cloudy apple juice

1 cup quinoa grain, rinsed and drained

1 green apple, cored and coarsely grated

1 red apple, cored and coarsely grated

zest of 1 orange

1 tbsp honey

1 tsp vanilla extract

Pour the apple juice in a large saucepan with the quinoa, apples, orange zest, honey and vanilla. Bring to the boil, then reduce the heat, cover and simmer for 15–20 minutes until the quinoa is soft and porridgey.

Serve with hot milk, an extra drizzle of honey and fresh fruit of your choice.

Creamy Cinnamon Pudding

Serves 4

I usually make this using full-cream milk as I prefer the rich creaminess. You can use the milk of your choice.

1 cup quinoa grain, rinsed and
    drained
1 cup water
¾ cup sugar
1½ tsp vanilla extract
4½ cups milk
ground cinnamon for dusting

Place the quinoa in a large saucepan with the water. Bring to the boil, then reduce the heat and simmer, covered, until most of the water has been absorbed, about 2–3 minutes.

Stir in the sugar and vanilla. Pour in the milk and bring to the boil, then reduce the heat and simmer, uncovered, for 20–30 minutes, stirring occasionally until the pudding is thick and creamy and the quinoa tender. Keep an eye on it as the milk can boil over.

Pour into individual serving bowls or one large bowl and sprinkle generously with cinnamon.

The pudding can be served hot, warm or cold. I like to leave it for about 30 minutes before serving it warm as it becomes even thicker as it stands.

Chocolate Cake

Serves 6

This cake remains moist and lasts for a few days.

1 tsp instant coffee powder

1 tsp hot water

4 eggs

¾ cup caster sugar

1 tsp vanilla extract

150gm (5oz) dark chocolate

½ cup quinoa flour

Icing

4 tbsp cocoa powder, sifted

75g (3oz) melted butter

3 cups icing sugar, sifted

3 tbsp hot water

Preheat the oven to 160ºC (310ºF).

Butter 2 x 20cm (8in) round cake tins and line the bottoms with baking paper; lightly butter the paper.

Dissolve the coffee in the hot water. Beat the eggs and sugar with an electric beater until light and fluffy, stir in the vanilla and the dissolved coffee.

Melt the chocolate in a bowl over hot simmering water, making sure that the bowl does not come in contact with the water. Cool slightly.

Mix the chocolate into the egg mixture, then fold in the flour.

Divide the mixture equally between the two cake tins and bake for about 15 minutes. Remove from the oven and leave in the tins for 5–10 minutes before turning out onto a wire rack to cool.

Prepare the icing by placing the cocoa in a bowl, stir in the butter and then the icing sugar, then add enough hot water to mix into a smooth spreading consistency.

When the cake is cold, sandwich the two halves together with a good layer of icing, then cover cake completely with the remaining icing. Decorate as desired.

Christmas Fruit Cake

Serves 8–10

This is a lovely Christmas cake and, being wheat- and gluten-free, it can be enjoyed by everyone. You need to start the cake the night before you intend to cook it.

125g (4oz) raisins
250g (8oz) sultanas
125g (4oz) currants
125g (4oz) mixed peel
90g (2oz) glace cherries, halved
juice of 1 orange
2 tbsp brandy
175g (6oz) unsalted butter
1 cup brown sugar, tightly packed
3 large eggs
1 cup quinoa flour
1 tsp ground cinnamon
1 tsp mixed spice
125g (4oz) blanched almonds, chopped
1 tbsp black treacle
2 tsp vanilla extract

Soak the raisins, sultanas, currants, mixed peel and cherries in the orange juice and brandy overnight. Stir once or twice if possible during the soaking time.

Preheat the oven to 125ºC (240ºF). Butter a 20cm (8in) round cake tin and line the bottom and sides with two layers of baking paper; the paper should be about 5cm (2in) above the sides.

Cream the butter and sugar until light and creamy, then beat in the eggs one at a time. Sift the flour, cinnamon and mixed spice and fold into the butter mixture, then gently mix in the soaked fruit with the soaking liquid, almonds, treacle and vanilla until thoroughly combined.

Spoon the cake mixture into the prepared tin, flatten the top evenly with a spatula or the back of a spoon and bake for 1½–1¾ hours, until the cake is lightly browned and cooked when tested with a metal skewer.

Allow to cool in the tin for at least 30 minutes before turning out onto a wire rack to cool completely.

Creamy Coconut and Mango Pudding

Serves 6–8

To toast the coconut flakes, place into a small non-stick frying pan and toast over a low heat—there's no need to add any oil or butter. This pudding is a favourite with everyone—it's absolutely delicious.

¾ cup quinoa grain, rinsed and
　　drained
2 x 400g (14oz) cans coconut milk,
　　plus extra ½ cup
¾ cup sugar
2 fresh mangoes
½ cup toasted coconut flakes

Place the quinoa in a large saucepan with all the coconut milk and the sugar. Bring to the boil, then reduce the heat, cover and simmer on low heat for 20–25 minutes, until thick and creamy.

Meanwhile, peel the mangoes. Thinly slice half of one to use as decoration later; set aside. Cut remaining mangoes into small pieces.

When the quinoa is soft and cooked, stir through the mango pieces and pour into individual bowls or a large serving bowl. Sprinkle with the toasted coconut and decorate with the slices of mango. Refrigerate before serving.

Basic Pancake Batter

Makes 6–8 pancakes

The buttermilk makes light and fluffy pancakes—you could use plain milk if you wish. These pancakes are wonderful with maple syrup or spread with your favourite jam.

1 cup quinoa flour
2 tbsp caster sugar
1 large egg
1½ cups buttermilk
1 tsp vanilla extract
butter for cooking

Sift the flour and sugar into a bowl.

Whisk the egg with the buttermilk and vanilla until combined; slowly pour into the flour, mixing with a whisk until you have a smooth batter.

Heat a small non-stick frying pan until hot, add a little butter to the pan and, when melted, pour in small ladlefuls of pancake mixture. Swirl the pan around to form an even pancake and cook on both sides until golden and set. Serve immediately.

VARIATION
For a savoury pancake, leave out the sugar and vanilla and season with salt and pepper instead. Mix in some cheese, cooked spinach, ham, corn or chorizo sausage.

Raspberry Muffins

Makes 12

You can replace the raspberries with any other frozen berries. Muffins are lovely eaten warm or cold and these ones will remain fresh and moist for three to four days.

2 cups quinoa flour

1¼ cups caster sugar

1 level tsp bicarbonate of soda

⅛ tsp salt

1 cup milk

2 large eggs

1½ tsp vanilla paste or extract

⅓ cup vegetable oil

175g (6oz) frozen raspberries

Preheat the oven to 180ºC (350ºF) and line a 12-cup muffin tin with 12 paper cases.

Sift together the flour, sugar, bicarbonate of soda and salt into a large bowl. Pour the milk into a jug, then lightly beat in the eggs, vanilla and oil.

Make a well in the centre of the dry ingredients and slowly pour in the liquid ingredients, mixing as you go until all the ingredients are combined. Gently fold in the frozen raspberries; do not over mix.

Spoon the mixture into the prepared muffin tin and bake for 30–35 minutes until the muffins have risen, are golden, firm to the touch and a skewer comes out clean when inserted into a muffin.

Leave to rest in the tin for 10–15 minutes before serving warm or placing on a wire rack to cool.

Pear Clafoutis

Serves 6

This is a light dessert and is best eaten while still warm. It is delicious any time of the year with cream or ice cream.

4 large ripe pears
60g (2oz) butter, melted
4 eggs
½ cup sugar, plus 2 Tbps
1 tsp vanilla bean paste or extract
¾ cup quinoa flour
2 cups full-fat milk
½ tsp nutmeg
icing sugar for dusting

Preheat the oven to 185°C (350°F).

Peel and core the pears, then thinly slice.

Use a little of the melted butter to grease a deep ovenproof tart dish, then pour the remaining butter over the pears and toss gently to coat each slice. Arrange the pear slices decoratively over the base of the dish. If you have extra slices just overlap them.

Beat the eggs and sugar with an electric beater until light and creamy, then stir in vanilla. Slowly add the flour and milk and continue mixing until combined.

Pour the mixture over the pears, sprinkle with nutmeg and bake for about 1–1¼ hours, until set and firm to the touch in the centre. Rest for 5–10 minutes before dusting with icing sugar and serving.

Rock Cakes

Makes 12–16

These are delicious with a cup of tea or coffee—they are crisp on the outside and moist and chewy inside.

1 cup quinoa flour

½ cup sugar, plus extra for
    sprinkling

1 tsp ground cinnamon

⅛ level tsp bicarbonate of soda

1 cup quinoa flakes

125g (4oz) butter, at room
    temperature

90g (3oz) sultanas

90g (3oz) mixed peel

½ cup milk

1 large egg

1 tsp vanilla extract

Preheat the oven to 175ºC (325ºF) and line a baking tray with baking paper.

Sift the flour, sugar, cinnamon and bicarbonate of soda into a bowl, then add the flakes and mix in well. Rub in the butter until mixture resembles coarse breadcrumbs. Mix in the sultanas and peel.

Whisk together the milk, egg and vanilla, pour into the flour mixture and lightly mix with a large spoon until the consistency is moist but stiff .

Put spoonfuls of the mixture onto the prepared baking tray and sprinkle each one with extra sugar. They should resemble rough heaps of dough. Bake for 15–20 minutes until golden and firm to the touch.

Pineapple, Banana and Walnut Cake

Serves 8–10

1½ cups quinoa flour

1¼ cups caster sugar

1 tsp ground cinnamon

3 eggs, lightly beaten

¾ cup vegetable oil or extra light
   olive oil

450g (1lb) can crushed pineapple,
   with juice

3 medium ripe bananas, mashed

90g (3oz) crushed walnuts or pecans,
   plus extra for decorating

1 tsp vanilla extract

Frosting

3 tbsp soft cream cheese

2 tbsp soft unsalted butter

1 tsp vanilla essence

1½ cups icing sugar, sifted

Preheat the oven to 175°C (340°F). Butter a 23cm (9in) square cake tin, preferably non-stick, line the bottom with baking paper; lightly butter the paper.

Sift the quinoa flour, sugar and cinnamon into a large bowl. Fold in the eggs, oil, pineapple and juice, bananas, nuts and vanilla. Stir until just combined.

Pour the cake mixture into the prepared cake tin and bake for 1–1¼ hours, until cooked. The cake should be golden and firm to the touch and a skewer should come out clean when inserted. Stand the cake in the tin for 10 minutes before turning onto a wire rack to cool.

To make the frosting, beat the cream cheese, butter and vanilla together, then slowly mix in the sifted icing sugar. Ice the cake with the frosting when completely cold and decorated with extra nuts.

Plum Tart

Serves 6–8

The tart is best served on the day it is made. You can chop the walnuts, then prepare the pastry dough in a food processor or a mixer, using a plastic blade. If you use steel blades, the walnuts will be too finely chopped.

125g (4oz) walnuts
2 cups quinoa flour
1 cup brown sugar, tightly packed
2 tsp vanilla extract
185g (7oz) unsalted butter at room
    temperature
1 large egg yolk
8 ripe plums, stoned, quartered
icing sugar for dusting (optional)

Preheat the oven to 170ºC (325ºF). Butter a 24cm (9½in) loose-bottom tart tin.

Finely chop the walnuts and place in a large mixing bowl. Add the flour, sugar, vanilla and mix well. Rub in the butter until the mixture starts coming together, then mix in the egg yolk. The dough should resemble a crumble mixture but hold together when pressed in your hand. Take out about 1 cup of the pastry and set aside.

Press the remaining dough tightly into the bottom and sides of the prepared tin. Arrange the plums, skin side down, decoratively over the base of the tart. Sprinkle the reserved walnut mixture over the top of the plums and bake for 30–40 minutes, until golden. Cool in the tin before gently loosening the sides and removing the tart from the tin. Sprinkle with icing sugar before serving if you wish.

NOTE
If plums are not in season, you can use 2 x 800g (28oz) cans of plums, drained well.

INDEX

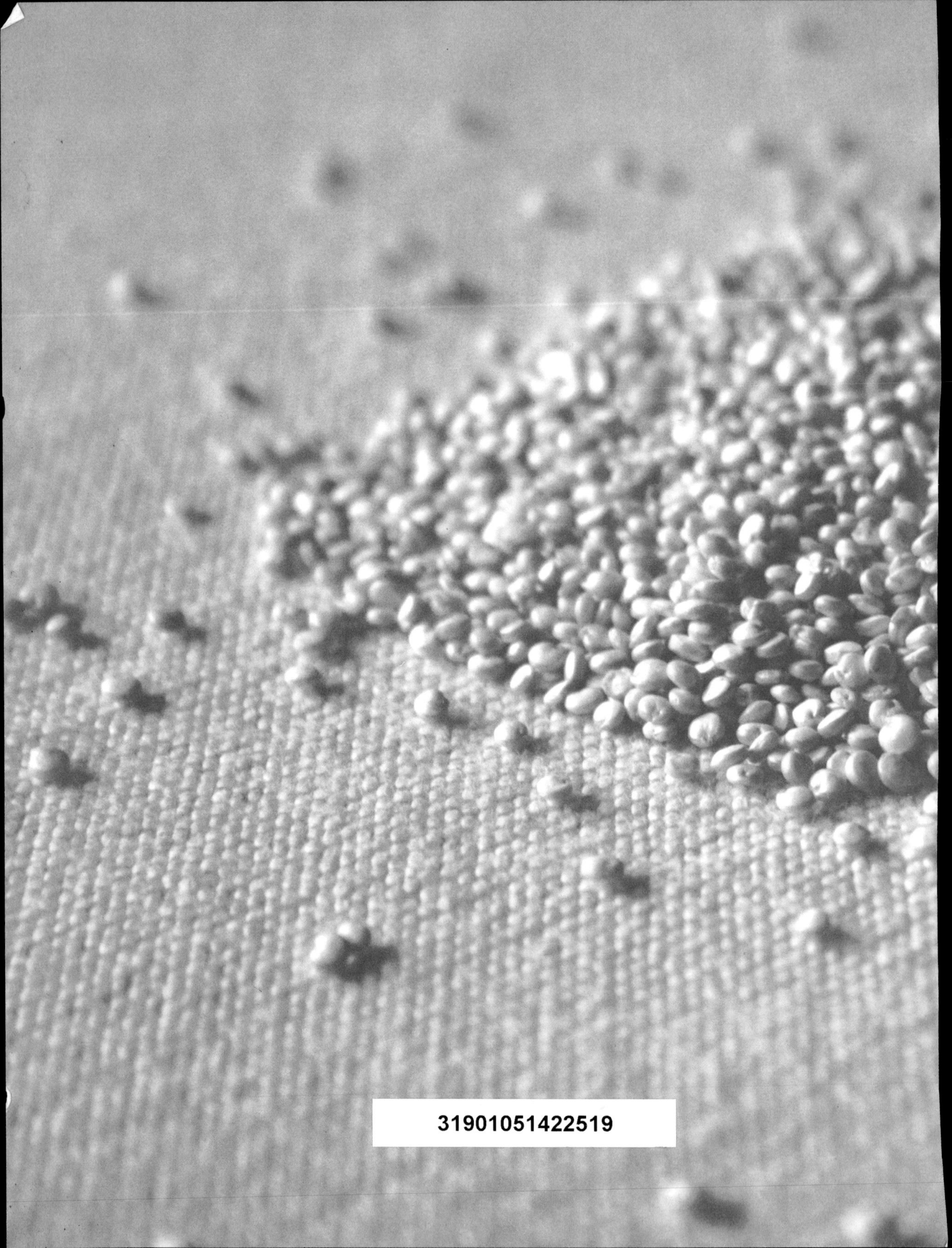